HOMEPLACE

HOMEPLACE

The Social Use and Meaning
of the Folk Dwelling in
Southwestern North Carolina

MICHAEL ANN WILLIAMS

University of Virginia Press
CHARLOTTESVILLE AND LONDON

University of Virginia Press
Originally published in 1991 by the University of Georgia Press
© 1991 by the University of Georgia Press
Printed in the United States of America on acid-free paper

First University of Virginia Press edition published 2004
ISBN 0-8139-2306-9 (paper)

9   8   7   6   5   4   3   2   1

Library of Congress Cataloging-in-Publication Data

Williams, Michael Ann.
  Homeplace : the social use and meaning of the folk dwelling in
southwestern North Carolina / Michael Ann Williams.-- 1st University of
Virginia Press ed.
     p. cm.
Originally published: Athens : University of Georgia Press, © 1991.
Includes bibliographical references and index.
  ISBN 0-8139-2306-9 (pbk. : alk. paper)
    1. Dwellings--North Carolina. 2. Vernacular architecture--North
Carolina. 3. Dwellings--Appalachian Region, Southern. 4. Vernacular
architecture--Appalachian Region, Southern. 5. North Carolina--Social
life and customs. I. Title.
GT225.N8W55 2004
392.3'6'09756--dc22

                                                            2003018810

To Mrs. Bennett
and her grandson, David

CONTENTS

ILLUSTRATIONS

ACKNOWLEDGMENTS

This book is a revised version of my doctoral dissertation completed in 1985 for the Department of Folklore and Folklife at the University of Pennsylvania. I thank my dissertation committee, especially Don Yoder and Chip Martin, for their support. A number of other people read early drafts and offered helpful comments and encouragement. Special thanks go to David Carpenter, Catherine Bishir, and Benita Howell.

The North Carolina Division of Archives and History lured me to southwestern North Carolina in the first place and its staff has been a continued source of encouragement and aid. Michael Southern, Martha Fullington, Nick Lanier, and (again and most especially) Catherine Bishir have all been helpful in many ways.

The Department of Geography, University of Illinois at Urbana-Champaign, provided me with an academic home away from home when I wrote my dissertation. My thanks to Geoffrey Hewings and John Jakle for making this possible.

A number of former and present graduate assistants in the Programs in Folk Studies at Western Kentucky University provided assistance in the revision and preparation of the manuscript. Thanks to Dawn Allen-Carlson, Daniel Carey, Sharon Celsor-Hughes, Carrie Helm, Amy Taylor, Mary Zwolinski, and especially, Ardell Jarratt. Also thanks go to

Karen Kallstrom, departmental secretary for the Department of Modern Languages and Intercultural Studies.

Kitty Manscill of the Sugarlands Visitor Center, Great Smoky Mountains National Park, Doug Day of the John C. Campbell Folk School, and the staffs of the Mountain Heritage Center at Western Carolina University and the Western Office of the North Carolina Division of Archives and History all helped to locate the photographs that illustrate this book. Their help was much appreciated.

My deepest gratitude goes to all the western North Carolinians who shared their memories with me. Their friendliness, frankness, and open hospitality never ceased to impress me. I hope this study does justice to the stories they had to tell.

Earlier versions of this work have appeared in three articles:

"The Little Big House: The Use and Meaning of the Single-Pen Dwelling," in *Perspectives in Vernacular Architecture, II* (Columbia: University of Missouri Press, 1986).

"Rethinking the House: Interior Space and Social Change," *Appalachian Journal* 14 (1987): 174–87. Reprinted in *Appalachian Images in Folk and Popular Culture,* edited by W. K. McNeil (Ann Arbor: UMI Research Press, 1989).

"Old Homeplace: Abandonment, Alteration, and the Multiple Purposes of the Dwelling," *Material Culture* 19, nos. 2–3 (1987).

An expansion of the material on boxed houses may be found in "Pride and Prejudice: The Appalachian Boxed House in Southwestern North Carolina," *Winterthur Portfolio* 25, no. 4 (Winter 1990).

HOMEPLACE

INTRODUCTION

Reinhabiting the House Through Narrative

Southwestern North Carolina is an ideal place to conduct a study of the social use and meaning of the folk house.[1] The folk dwellings of this region are not artifacts of a distant past. People are readily available to tell us how these homes were used and what they meant to the individuals who lived within them.

Several factors create this availability of oral testimony. One is the remarkably conservative nature of folk building in the region. The use of traditional architectural plans and techniques persisted well into the twentieth century. This conservatism is coupled with a cultural tendency toward rebuilding rather than retention of folk dwellings. While folk building traditions survived over a long period of time, individual structures, on a whole, did not. The majority of extant folk structures in southwestern North Carolina were built during a period still knowable through oral history. Other folk dwellings that have not survived to the present day still live in the memories of many older western Carolinians.

By focusing on the intangible as well as tangible aspects of the folk house, oral testimony allows us to examine the complex relationship between people and their dwellings. Listening to people's experience of the dwelling reveals aspects of this relationship that are not know-

Figure 1. Oral testimony is a useful tool in understanding the social and symbolic use of folk dwellings in southwestern North Carolina. Meadows House, 1882, Buncombe County, N.C. (North Carolina Division of Archives and History, Western Office; photograph by Mary Jo Brezny).

able through looking at the structures alone. For many folk building traditions, the structures, or scarce documents, are all we have left. Southwestern North Carolina gives us a rare opportunity to know folk buildings through the testimony of individual experience.

The purpose of this study is twofold. By reconstructing how rural dwellings were used and what they meant to their inhabitants, we might better understand the folk building tradition and its cultural context in one distinct region of Appalachia. The late nineteenth century to early twentieth century, the period of folk building best understood through oral history, was a time of immense social and economic change in Appalachia. By examining something as fundamental as rural housing, we can better reconstruct the nature of everyday life in this region during this period of change.

On a more abstract level, the purpose is to examine the extent to which the use and meaning of dwellings are revealed in physical form. If we are to "read" buildings as cultural artifacts, we need to understand as fully as possible the complex relationship of how buildings are used, socially and symbolically, and how buildings are physically constructed, altered, preserved, or destroyed. The availability of oral testimony provides one means to examine this subject through specific case studies. The goal is to enhance our understanding of the complexity of the relationship between the use of the dwelling and its physical form and to suggest where caution must be used in our interpretations of domestic structures as artifacts. Conclusions of this nature, however, must be limited; the specific uses accounted for in this study do not prove interpretations of folk dwellings in other regions true or false and the specific uses (particularly of certain house types) in southwestern North Carolina should not be applied by analogy to similar structures in other regions.

The benefits of conducting this study in southwestern North Carolina were not limited to the longevity of its traditional building system and the corresponding availability of oral testimony. Due to a state program of comprehensive architectural survey, sponsored by the North Carolina Division of Archives and History, the folk architecture of the region has been well documented. The information derived from these surveys provides the base on which this study was built.[2] In a sense, however, the conception for this study grew from the need to deal with unsolicited information. The questions I asked were for the most part inspired by sixteen months of architectural survey I conducted in southwestern North Carolina. As I began my first eight-month survey (of Henderson County) I saw oral history primarily as a useful tool for understanding the histories of individual structures. I soon found that people could tell you far more than who built what, when. It was particularly those bits of information which defied my expectations that troubled me into pursuing oral history further. As I began my eight-month survey of Cherokee County, I started to ask specific questions and to keep a better record of the responses.

In order to confront the issues that arose from my experience in Henderson and Cherokee counties, I decided to focus my attention on people rather than on structures. During the final stage of my research, I conducted interviews with approximately fifty individuals who were born in or lived in rural southwestern North Carolina during the late nineteenth or early twentieth centuries. Although a few individuals still lived in or near their old homes, the majority did not. For most of the individuals interviewed, the homeplace now only existed in memories.

The choice not to interview individuals only in reference to specific extant structures had several advantages. For one, it avoided the biases inherent in the variable survivability of different types of dwellings. This is particularly important in a region where permanence was not a building priority among a large sector of the population. Oral history indicated a far more conservative pattern of building and use than is suggested by surviving structures. Secondly, interviewing people about their memory of the dwelling encouraged them to focus on the experiential rather than on the tangible aspects of architecture. Most people did not remember a house, they remembered a home. Finally, without a structure to examine, I was forced to listen carefully rather than look, training my ears as well as my eyes. Sometimes, I found, people contradicted rather than corroborated the physical evidence.

The limited reach of oral history made this a study of folk architecture in transition. Although many individuals were able to pass on some valuable information about previous generations, they spoke most eloquently of their own experience. Where there would be several advantages to studying a more vital and stable folk tradition, studying the effects of cultural change is not without its merits. An architectural tradition in decline perhaps better reveals the connections and disjunctions of systems of use, systems of meaning, and systems of building. As I was to find, changes in one system do not necessarily entail changes

Figure 2. Conservative retention of building traditions: man making pun-cheons, 1937 (Great Smoky Mountains National Park).

in another; in fact, they often operate to counterbalance the effects of tradition and change.

The experiences of the individuals interviewed greatly shaped the nature of the study. The majority were users, not builders, of folk architecture. Many lived in folk houses as children but not as adults, and their memories are of a child's view of the folk house. From firsthand experience, these individuals are able to contrast the patterns of spatial use practiced during their childhood by their parents and grandparents with the patterns of spatial use witnessed in their own adult lives. These perspectives allow us to better understand folk architecture from the experience of the dweller.

The visitor to southwestern North Carolina who ventures into rural communities might find many popular stereotypes dispelled. The "mountaineer" has often been portrayed as suspicious or hostile to strangers. In rural southwestern North Carolina, I was frequently surprised at how many doors opened readily, how often hospitality was extended. As I sat and listened to individuals' memories of the past, I discovered that in many families it was once unthinkable to turn away a stranger. Even today, individuals living in the most isolated communities tend to be the most likely to welcome the stranger.

As I began my surveys, I was cautioned by some townspeople who questioned the wisdom of going alone into the more remote areas. However, early on, an old man who lived in a mountainous section of Henderson County assured me that it was safe "up here with us" (though I should watch my step down in town). I did most of the fieldwork alone, without incident. My own trust was encouraged by the way people seemed to trust me, seldom hesitating to let me in the front door. Perhaps the fact that I was a woman, alone, helped, but I believe the traditional ethic of welcoming strangers was also still in operation. In one spontaneous fieldwork encounter, I was sent to meet a woman in her nineties who lived alone. Midway through the interview, she mused that perhaps it was not the smartest thing these days to invite a total stranger into her house. After all, she "didn't know me from Adam's housecat." But she had invited me in, and I doubt that she had any real intention of changing her ways.

For the most part, people found it unremarkable that I should want to tape record their memories. I usually tried to pre-arrange meetings by telephone, but few rural people treated arriving unannounced as inappropriate behavior. In fact, the most frequent response to a phone call to arrange a date and time for an interview was "come on over." In cases where I did arrive unannounced, usually because the person did not have a phone or the encounter was spontaneous, individuals were no less responsive. One morning I visited a woman who lived miles from her nearest neighbor, without a phone or a means of transportation. Before I could properly get out my intent in visiting, she enlisted me in solving the problem of why her refrigerator had just quit working. After an hour of fussing with fuses, electrical outlets, and extension cords, we solved the problem. She then turned to me and asked, "Now what is it I can do for you?" I spent the rest of the day interviewing her and left, declining an invitation to spend a few nights. While some individuals took a bit of convincing, the open hospitality was common, particularly among those who had remained in their rural communities all their lives.

Most of the individuals I interviewed had not been formally interviewed before. However, frequently I received the impression that a person had just been waiting for a stranger with a tape recorder to show up. Perhaps for some this expectation may have been shaped by the number of folklorists in the past who had found the region a happy hunting ground or by the popularity of *Foxfire* and local-color writers. But many were unaware of these publications or the discipline of folklore. They were aware that they had witnessed vast changes in their lifetime, and they logically assumed that someone should want to hear their story. They "studied on" past experiences and most of the narratives I heard had been told before, if not recorded.

The majority of interviews took place in private homes. This stage of my fieldwork took me into modern ranch houses, small apartments, mobile homes, and in a few cases older, traditional dwellings. I made

notes on contemporary spatial use of these current homes, but the
most striking fact was that, despite the very conservative pattern of
use during the early twentieth century, so little visible evidence remains of traditional spatial use. While observation of contemporary
social and symbolic use may have potential for future studies, I found
listening to memories of the past a greater source of understanding
traditional architectural use and meaning. Individuals who grew up in
late nineteenth-century or early twentieth-century southwestern North
Carolina witnessed incredible changes in their lifetimes. Although some
are nostalgic for the past, and a few believe they are now living "close
to the end of time," the majority seem remarkably at home in today's
world. The woman who described spending evenings as a young child
picking words from the newspapers that papered the inside of her
family's log house was chatting on a cordless phone when I arrived. A
gentleman, in his nineties, switched from talking fondly of the past to
speaking of his enthusiasm for the Democrats' choice of a female vice-
presidential candidate. Many in their everyday life delicately balanced
old and new ways. Anna Collett was bleaching apples the day I came
to visit. In her kitchen was a wood burning cook stove, in use, and a
microwave oven.

*TRADITION
+
CONVENIENCE*

No ideal informant exists who can best lead us to traditional architectural use and meaning. The individuals interviewed for this study came
from a variety of social and economic backgrounds. All had different
stories to tell. Among those interviewed were a number with a minimum
of formal education, though this did not prevent them from eloquently
describing their pasts. Rich portraits of the past were also created by
the retired college professor who had spent most of her adult life outside the region. I interviewed individuals who grew up on prospering
river valley farms and those who grew up in isolated narrow valleys.
Some never left their home communities; others were lured or were un-
willingly pulled from the region during parts of their childhood or adult
life. Larry Gunter's family moved temporarily to Tennessee and Kentucky when he was a child so that his father could work in the mines,
and Robert Blanton's family moved briefly to Gastonia, North Caro-

lina, to be near the mills. Grady Carringer spent much of his adult life working in the industrial north. Both Kate Rogers and Addie Norton followed their husbands to the state of Washington, and then returned home. Gilford Williams served in the Pacific during World War II. I met some who had no desire ever to see what lay outside their own county, others who were well traveled. Monroe Ledford shared with me his detailed memories of the past and his photographs and souvenirs from a recent trip to Alaska.

Neither education nor lack of it, mobility nor stability makes the individual's memories richer. For some the past is meaningful because they feel its continuity in their present lives. For others, the past has been thrown into relief by the changes that have occurred in their lives. Some actively sought change; others resisted or were its reluctant victims. Some remember good old days, others harsh realities. Most were ambivalent about the changes they experienced.

Absolute age did not necessarily affect the nature of changes perceived by those interviewed. Between the 1880s and 1930s change came at various speeds to different families and communities. As I was particularly interested in this time period, the majority of individuals interviewed were over the age of seventy (Table 1). Fourteen were born before 1900. Of the four younger than seventy, R. O. Wilson was the youngest. I chose to interview him because of his interest in and knowledge of traditional construction. As it turned out, he also could reconstruct his family's building history back to the Civil War. Similar to many men, R.O. saw architectural change primarily in terms of construction technique. As he thought about it, however, he began to recognize traditional patterns of spatial use in his own family's use of space. "You know," he observed after an interview, "the way we lived down there [in his circa 1920s homeplace below his current house] was not so different from the way my grandparents lived in that log house."

My intention in my fieldwork was to understand folk architecture in relation to its users, women as well as men. The heavy preponderance of women among those interviewed, however, was initially unintended. Of the individuals of the age and background I was interested in, I simply

Table 1. Age and Gender Distribution
of Individuals Interviewed

Birth Date	Women	Men	Total
1881–85	1	0	1
1886–90	1	1	2
1891–95	4	2	6
1896–1900	7	2	9
1901–5	4	0	4
1906–10	11	5	16
1911–15	6	3	9
1916–20	1	1	2
1921–25	0	0	0
1926–30	0	0	0
1931–35	0	1	1
Total	35	15	50

Note: Post survey interviews only are included.

found more women than men. However, I soon found that women were generally more articulate and insightful about the use of interior domestic space. Most men seemed more comfortable discussing the physical rather than the social and symbolic dimensions of architecture.[3]

It is no surprise that women would more intimately know the interior arrangements of the house. However, I also found that one could not stereotype women's domestic roles as confined to the interior of the dwelling. Division of labor, and space, by sex was not always so strict. Women and girls in many families participated in agricultural work beyond just gardening, including working in the fields, and many actively preferred outdoor work. Girls in large families could sometimes choose between outdoor and indoor work. Even adult women in some cases chose to spend a high percentage of their time working outdoors. Still, I found even those women who expressed their preference for the outside were articulate about the patterns of interior spatial use. Perhaps women, freed from the role of builders, have generally had the opportunity to think more abstractly about architecture, or they simply think

Figure 3. R. O. Wilson, Jackson County, N.C. (Mountain Heritage Center, Western Carolina University).

of houses in their social dimension. I do not want to imply that all men were incapable of talking about internal space; a few were excellent sources of information. Generally, however, men tended to be a good bit more knowledgeable about how houses were put together than what went on inside them.

The most difficult task in analyzing the experiences of those I interviewed was to characterize their shared experience without discounting the unique aspects of each individual's life. While collective patterns may be found, they should not be used to stereotype the experience of any single individual. On the other hand, I have avoided using certain individuals' lives as case studies, particularly where it involved dwelling on personal data not specifically relevant to the focus of my study. While inclusion of this data might be justified as a concern for "context," I do not wish to overstep any boundaries of privacy of those individuals who were kind enough to share their experiences.

Of course, the various individuals interviewed contributed in varying degrees to the study. Some corroborated information on regional patterns, others provided small but vital pieces of the puzzle, and a few were instrumental in my overall understanding of social and symbolic use of folk houses in southwestern North Carolina. Of the latter group, I would like to give special recognition to four individuals: the gentlemanly and articulate Monroe Ledford and three women of humor and strength, Kate Rogers, Zena Bennett, and Eller Garrett. This is their story, but it also belongs to the many others who contributed their narratives.

After many months of collecting these rich and diverse narratives, I was faced with the problem of understanding what they meant. How are these memories of the experience of the house to be understood and evaluated? Material and oral evidence, it would seem, could simply be "tested" against each other. Tangible artifacts with vague meanings are weighed against intangible, but explicit, memories. History is derived from the interpretation of one and

Figure 4. Kate Rogers, Macon County, N.C. (Photograph by the author).

the evaluation of the other. Houses and oral history, however, are more than categories of evidence from which we derive facts. Both are forms of cultural expression. Between the narrative and the physical form of the house are the meanings and behaviors that shape the form of the house and the experience contained within, or attached to, the house. In order to study houses through narrative form, we need to first come to some understanding of their relationship.

This study presupposes various "systems" of architectural use. For the individual, however, these systems exist only through experience and most people do not verbally abstract these systems away from experience. Rather, individuals use narrative to "reinhabit" the house— to order and comment on the experiential aspects of the house, thereby evoking past systems of social use and cultural meaning.

With the exception of some builders, the majority of people do not talk abstractly even about the physical form of the house. The form of the house is often remembered through the memory of specific experiences.[4] Frances Bryson, for instance, recalled the layout of her childhood home through her memory of a childhood illness: "The kitchen and the dining room was, we had to come out on the porch to get into the kitchen and dining room. We all had the measles at home and it was kind of cold and I remember my daddy he'd take us in one at a time for a meal. He'd put a coat around us and bring us out on the porch and go in the kitchen and dining room."[5]

During the course of one interview, a woman who was an avid narrator seemed inclined to talk about anything except the house in which she was raised and now lives. Eventually it became apparent that it was not that she was reluctant to talk about the house, but that she was searching for the proper narrative in which to talk about it. Midway through the interview she launched into a lengthy story about a storm that hit the house, a narrative that had many details about the house and the layout of the farmstead.

> Now to prove to you how strong this house was, in twenty-three, the year before Aunt Kate Hall died, one hot evening,

just about like this. It was in early fall, I guess along about the first of September. And all this Rose Creek tribe over here, who lived here, have to come across through this gap, and walk down through the lot here and go over to West Mill. . . . They'd always holler and say "Miss Kate," she'd be setting in that old log kitchen door, achurning, you know, old timey churn like that, lots of morning, "we'll bring you your mail."

Well along up in the evening, I don't think any of them eat dinner here that day. It had rained that morning. Somebody, a crowd of them passed through here. Well they come back about two o'clock and handed in some papers. . . .

And Granny, and Aunt Kate, and I were sitting right in there at that old big chimney, at the fireplace, in that old log kitchen.

. . . the ladies went on, they said, "we'd better hurry, it's storming and getting worse" and they went on across the mountain.

Wasn't anybody here but us.

And up an hour, maybe, after they left, it just suddenly got dark. And it was just so hot that you couldn't hardly stand it.

Well, all at once, it just come up this awfullest gust of wind. Only time I ever saw Aunt Kate Hall cry. . . .

Well Aunt Kate, as the wind hit here, she stepped to the door.

And, I don't know whether she'd even seen a cedar tree blown up or not. But it came right down, headed toward the house, right by the end of the crib shed (as the shed was a circular thing around the old crib).

Well she turned and she always called Grandmother, her sister, she'd say, "Sister Lizie." She said, "Law, Sister Lizie, storm's hitting."

Well about that time, there was a huge poplar tree, stood in the back. Well twenty-five or thirty feet of it, the top of it laid over that kitchen and dining room, now. Now, that log kitchen and dining room roof. Never broke the roof or nothing, it laid over it.

Well, Aunt Kate got excited. She ran through the kitchen, there was a door on each side, and looked. . . .

Well, Aunt Kate turned around and went to crying. She said, "Sister Lizie, it looks like our home's going to be blowed away."

Well I was a little old child about eight, nine years old. I ran through here, and as it happened now they didn't have any screen doors. They had a door just similar to that right there where that last window is, going out on the porch. And that door happened to be closed that evening.

Well, I ran through here, we have that fireplace smaller than what it was then, just as I passed there, several bricks rolled down on the floor.

Well I ran and jerked that door open. It opened back. There was a huge bed, it was made very much like that bed, that Miss Ethel Massey gave me. . . .

Well, I went to screaming, "Granny, Aunt Kate, here's a big tree across the house."

There was a pine tree, much bigger than any you see here now, and the men who took it off the house said that they took off about fifty feet of it. The top of it had come across the upstairs porch, over here on to the, over across the ridge pole of this house, and had only broken one post, corner post, down there. Now [my husband] described how the upstairs posts were put together.

It broke that post and the railing off, had old banisters, you know, up and down the railing that away. And it broke some of the ridge pole, right up here, and kind of crushed in the corner of the upstairs room.

Well they didn't believe me. I went to screaming and a hollering. To come here, to come here, "the big pine tree's on the porch," I said, just a little old young'un excited.

And Aunt Kate, I remember just as well as anything, when she'd come through; now that kitchen and dining room, you stepped up six inches from the big house, from those two rooms.

Well she come in such a hurry she nearly fell as she come through that door. I imagine that had been a little walkway between the kitchen and the big house, like you see, and they had closed that up to make a dining room, modern.

Well anyhow, when Aunt Kate got in here, there was another brick or two.

Well she was just shocked to death. And the limbs were sticking in that door, now, of the pine tree. Well she couldn't get the door shut. . . .

Well she had, she was standing there looking at them limbs now, they's plumb inside the door and me and Granny standing with her.

And Granny says, "Well it must have torn down the chimney."

There's, her rocking chair's asetting right over there in the corner of the chimney and she went over there and set down. Course she was more feeble, she was older than Aunt Kate.

And Aunt Kate was asaying, "Well what will we do, Sister Lizie, what will we do. We can't close the door."

After continuing on, Katherine Porter ended with this coda: "And that was one of the most exciting things that happened to me; Aunt Kate died the next year in March. But that was one of the most exciting things that ever happened in regard to this old house. So you know it's bound to be strong."

To the narrator, the house was not a physical entity to be described logically; it was part of her experience and she described it within the context of experience. She chose a narrative that expressed her feelings about the nature of her house (its endurance and strength) and she keyed its occurrence in time to other important life events (the death of her great-aunt).[6]

While most people do not talk about house form and use abstractly, some people use their own experience to think about houses abstractly. Experiences are individualistic, but they characterize shared systems of use and form. In some cases, though, experiences are also shared and find repeated expression in narrative form. The repeated appearance of narrative content should not necessarily make us question the veracity of the individual's account. Instead, we might wonder why it appears to be such a key experience.

Houses have many functions, but at their most elemental they protect their inhabitants from the environment. This forms our most basic definition of the house. Nature, however, had the power to violate the protection folk houses of southwestern North Carolina offered. Stories about violations of the distinctions between inside and outside abound. Wildlife found its way inside: "Snakes would come in on you just anywhere they wanted to. I looked up one morning and got up and a big old black snake, he was just licking his tongue out sort of like that. Course, a black snake wouldn't hurt you, unless he choke you to death or something."[7] Chickens and other livestock could be seen through the cracks in the floor boards of some houses. Other stories took on less believable proportions, such as stories of houses with cracks in the exterior wall so large "you could throw a cat through" (a common regional saying).[8] One man told a story about his young son rolling over in bed one night and waking to find himself out in the yard.[9] Whether these stories are true or false, they provide a means for the individual to think about, and talk about, the nature of the house.

One of the stories about houses told most frequently in southwestern North Carolina concerns the individual waking up to discover snow on the bed covers. Variations of the story occur over and over again. This narrative is generally not told as a hardship story. In fact, people usually assert that they were not cold. Instead, the story is most often told with the sense of awe that a child must feel when awakening to discover himself or herself blanketed with snow. The fact that the story is repeated so often suggests that it was not only a common experience, but that it

Figure 5. James R. Reagan place in the snow (Photograph ca. 1930; Great Smoky Mountains National Park).

was an important experience for many people.[10] What better symbol of the violation of the protective function of the dwelling is there than the ability of nature to blanket the inside of the house with snow?[11]

People contemplate the way houses used to be and how they have changed. Aspects of the house, such as the ease with which nature violated the physical protection of the house, once accepted as natural, now cause people to wonder. "And I've seen it you could look right up through the top of the house and see the light. And I've seen it come a big snow. I've seen it blow in on the beds. [Laughs.] Now that's about, now that's something else. And course, we didn't pay a bit of attention to it then. And now, I've often studied how people lived and survived and got by." [12] Experience narratives provide a means for individuals to focus their memories on the details of the house, and they provide a way for people to ponder the nature of the house and how it has changed.

Scholars of artifacts often find old houses frustrating. We know that they represent many uses and many meanings, but these uses and meanings are not fully crystalized in physical forms. Once houses are emptied of human habitation, their complexities are not easily read. Former inhabitants also find these empty shells inadequate representations of home. The physical form does not fully represent the experiences and meanings attached to the home.

The fluidity of the narrative form, on the other hand, has the ability to give expression to these intangible aspects of the dwelling. Old houses and homesites evoke powerful memories. Narratives give these memories a more tangible form. They organize past experience and they empower the teller to share memories with others. The "old homeplace" is a potent symbol in southwestern North Carolina. The homeplace, however, is often "preserved" through narrative rather than through the physical rehabilitation of the structure itself.

The oral testimonies presented in this study are not simple answers to a list of questions. As many people say, they "study on" their past experiences, and they preserve these experiences by telling them over and over again. The narratives are not memories of artifacts, once removed from the real thing; they constitute direct evidence in and of themselves. They are important, not because they help us reconstruct physical forms that no longer exist, but because they give form to the intangible, experiential aspects of architecture.

CHAPTER ONE

People and Place

For the purpose of this study, southwestern North Carolina consists of the eleven westernmost counties of the state. This region is part of the Appalachian Summit, the highest and most southern section of the Appalachian mountain system. A roughly triangular region, southwestern North Carolina is bordered on the east by the Blue Ridge and on the northwest by the Great Smoky Mountains. A number of rivers cut through this mountainous region; among the largest are the Hiwassee, Little Tennessee, Pigeon, and French Broad, all tributaries of the Tennessee River. While the river valleys are not wide, they are fertile. The region is blessed with a moderate climate: cool summers and relatively mild winters.

According to archaeological evidence, southwestern North Carolina has supported human habitation since the Paleo-Indian period, approximately twelve thousand years ago. By the time of European contact, this region was the heartland of the Cherokee Nation, whose influence spread far into adjoining regions. In the late seventeenth century, regular trade relationships were established between the Cherokee of this region and European settlers further east.[1] White settlement of southwestern North Carolina, however, lagged well behind the rest of the state. By the time this section was fully open to white settlers, the country's frontier had already pushed considerably west of the Appalachians. Along

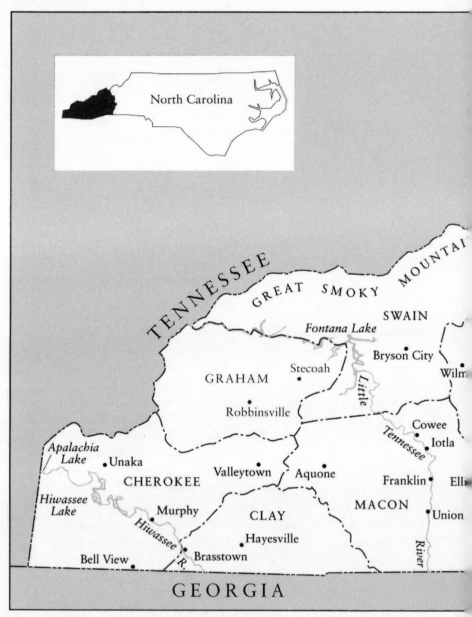

Figure 6. Study area: the eleven westernmost counties of North Carolina

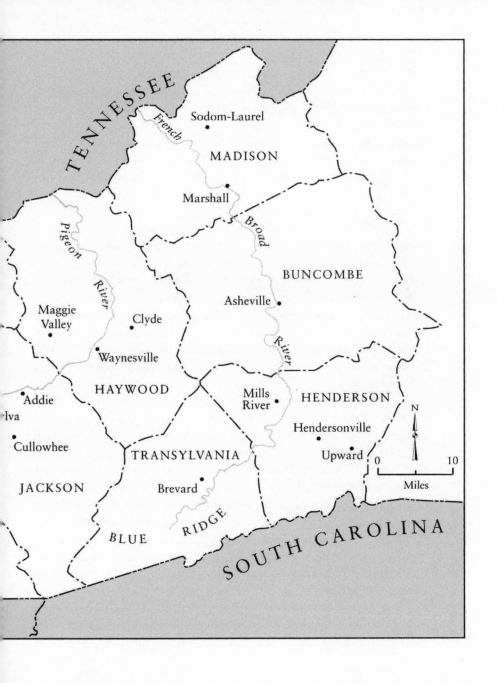

with the rugged terrain, it was the powerful presence of the Cherokee Nation that impeded white settlement. At the beginning of the American Revolution, the Cherokee still claimed all of this region. In subsequent decades their claim was slowly eroded, but it was not until 1835 that the Treaty of New Echota sealed the fate of the North Carolina Cherokee. The western quarter of the region (present-day Cherokee, Graham, and Clay counties) was opened to white settlement in 1838, following the forced removal of the majority of the Cherokees to Oklahoma.

Ironically, it was the Cherokee who first brought elements of European-derived folk architecture to southwestern North Carolina. At the time of contact, the traditional dwellings of the Cherokee were square or occasionally circular structures of wattle-and-daub construction.[2] During the eighteenth century the Cherokee abandoned traditional techniques in the building of dwellings in favor of horizontal log construction, which they possibly learned from the white traders. Philadelphia naturalist William Bartram described log houses built by the North Carolina Cherokee in 1776: "The Cherokees construct their habitations on a different plan from the Creeks; that is, but one oblong four square building, of one story high; the materials consisting of logs or trunks of trees, stripped of their bark, notched at their ends, fixed one upon another, and afterwards plaistered well, both inside and out, with clay well tempered with dry grass, and the whole covered or roofed with the bark of the chestnut tree or long broad shingles."[3]

During this period the Cherokees were still building round ceremonial and civic structures using their traditional forms of construction. Approximately half a century later, a report in the *Missionary Gazetteer* stated that the Cherokee lived "mostly, in log-cabins, not much inferior to those of the whites in neighboring settlements."[4] In fact, some settlers moved directly into Cherokee structures after the Removal. The families of those Cherokee who eluded removal or were permitted to stay continued to build houses that were physically undifferentiated from those of their white neighbors. An example of a nineteenth-century Cherokee log dwelling is found in the Boiling Springs community of Chero-

Figure 7. Cherokee family in front of log house, Swain County, N.C., 1936
(Great Smoky Mountains National Park).

kee County. Oral history, supported by documentary evidence, suggests that the house was built by John Axe. It is quite possible, however, that the Cherokee maintained patterns of spatial use within these Anglo-American house types that were quite different from those of the white settlers, but this question awaits further research.

Southwestern North Carolina shares a folk architectural tradition with all of the Upland South of the United States. This subregion was a direct heir to the cultural fusions of English, Irish, and Germanic building practices that took place in Pennsylvania and western Virginia. Many of the early white settlers, or their families, followed the classic settlement route from southeast Pennsylvania to the Valley of Virginia, to piedmont North Carolina, and then into the mountains of western Carolina. Other settlers came from the south, migrated west across North Carolina, or entered from Tennessee.

Ethnic differences in the building of folk architecture were never pronounced in southwestern North Carolina despite the mixture of ethnic backgrounds of the early white settlers. A quarter to over a half of the early white population were of Scotch-Irish descent; other settlers were of English, German, French, and Welsh origin.[5] By the time white settlement was fully established in the region, a new Anglo-American architecture had eclipsed Old World house types in the Upland South. Germanic heritage is found primarily in the prevalence of horizontal log construction; while found in some parts of piedmont North Carolina and western Virginia, German house plans are not found in southwestern North Carolina. Rather, the system of house plans, derived primarily from English and Irish antecedents, was American in its use of a modular system of rectangular units.

The common folk house types of rural southwestern North Carolina are typical of those generally found in the Upland South. The square, or more frequently rectangular, single pen house, with all its variants, was probably the most common folk house type of southwestern North Carolina during the nineteenth century.[6] At its most basic, the single pen house was a small one-room cabin; in larger versions of the plan the main room was sometimes partitioned, and the house often had an upstairs or loft and a separate kitchen.

Of the larger folk houses, the saddlebag plan with its rooms of equal size on either side of a central chimney was the most prevalent. Again, the saddlebag house often had an upstairs (usually the house was a story and a half, rather than a full two stories in height) and a separate kitchen. The double pen house with exterior end chimneys is considerably less common, though examples can be found. The dogtrot house, common in some parts of the Upland South, is also relatively rare. This plan consists of two units of equal size separated by an (originally) open central passage. Extant examples in southwestern North Carolina are of log, and all their central passages have been enclosed. Most people who recall a "dogtrot" actually remember a single pen house connected to a kitchen by a roofed walkway rather than a true dogtrot plan.

Of the common folk house types of the Upland South, the center-passage I-house alone owes a significant part of its ancestry to the high style. In southwestern North Carolina, the coming of the Georgian-derived I-house was connected to the growing social and economic diversity of the region during the decades before the Civil War. As trade and transportation developed, individuals with large holdings of river valley land prospered. Along the valleys of the French Broad, Little Tennessee, and Hiwassee rivers, in particular, landowners, most of them slave holders, built center-passage I-houses during the 1840s and 1850s. After the Civil War, center-passage houses tended to be more modest in size, but they were never as common as elsewhere in North Carolina.[7]

The folk house plan is commonly, though not invariably, linked to construction technique. Single pen houses were usually built of log, I-houses of frame, and saddlebags of either, though frame was preferred during the late nineteenth century. However, it was not uncommon for single pen log dwellings to be expanded by frame additions into double pen plan or center-passage houses. Log construction frequently reflected the efforts of unpaid community cooperation while frame houses were more often the product of hired labor.

During most of the nineteenth century the economic base of south-western North Carolina was predominantly agricultural. The builders of center-passage I-houses were settled on rich bottomland and had the greatest access to commercial markets. These western Carolinians were also most likely to be involved in some non-agricultural enterprises. The dwellers of the smaller folk houses were more likely to live on small family farms clustered in relatively self-sufficient communities. While these rural communities were not totally isolated, either economically, socially, or politically, they tended to rely within the community on a barter system and the cooperative exchange of labor. This communal system supported the agricultural base of the community, as well as the continuity of a folk architectural tradition.

Until the late nineteenth century, the physical resources of Appalachia were largely left unexploited. The physical beauty of western North Carolina attracted wealthy visitors to the region as early as the 1820s, following the completion of the Buncombe Turnpike. Looking to escape the heat of summer, rich lowlanders (particularly South Carolinians) built summer homes at Flat Rock and other communities accessible to the turnpike. Their homes starkly contrasted to local building norms. By the end of the nineteenth century, as transportation to the region improved, tourism expanded and was no longer limited to the very rich. Today, it remains a crucial part of the region's economy.

The building of the railroad in southwestern North Carolina was delayed not only by the mountainous terrain but also by the social and economic disruptions of the postbellum period. Chartered before the Civil War, the railroad was not constructed in southwestern North Carolina until the 1880s. As in the rest of Appalachia, long delayed industrialization followed close behind the coming of the railroad. Lacking the rich deposits of coal, southwestern North Carolina was spared some of the social and economic trauma inflicted upon the mining regions of central Appalachia. However, while not a coal region, southwestern North Carolina was rich in Appalachia's other great natural resource, timber. What began as small-scale family operations providing additional income to farmers became by the turn of the century a major industrial

Figure 8. Steam engine in front of log railroad station, Aquone, N.C. (Mountain Heritage Center, Western Carolina University).

Figure 9. Champion Fibre Company Sawmill, Smokemont, N.C., 1933 (Great Smoky Mountains National Park).

enterprise. Huge sections of land were purchased by interests outside the region. Although relatively short-lived, the timber boom had a major impact on the economic and social life of the region.[8]

The coming of the railroad also brought architectural change to southwestern North Carolina. In towns, conservative use of Victorian style elements was common in the late nineteenth century and the use of traditional house plans declined rapidly after the turn of the century. The relatively small number of rural folks who prospered during this period (especially those in Buncombe County and Madison County who were a part of a boom in flue-cured tobacco) also experimented with Victorian style, applying ornamental trim to their traditional houses and gently breaking away from the confinements of a traditional plan.

Architectural change came much more slowly for the majority of rural people in southwestern North Carolina. A prolonged period of slow change, dating from the 1880s to the 1930s, characterized the building practices of the rural majority. During this period many rural people were drawn for the first time to "public work" (paid employment away from home), which was found primarily in timber or related industries. While many men began to work away from home, families strove to maintain their rural lifestyles and community ties. Women were often left to run the family farm. As the timber boom tapered off, many rural individuals, now dependent on the cash economy, were forced even farther from home, often outside the region, to look for paid work. Many left permanently; others only sojourned, returning eventually to their rural communities after working in the textile mills of piedmont Carolina, the coal fields of West Virginia or Kentucky, the factories of the industrial north, or the lumber camps of the timber-rich Pacific northwest.[9]

The folk architecture of this transitional period reflected constraints imposed on the available time of rural builders by their participation in the cash economy. Although many rural communities continued to work cooperatively at house building, neighbors simply had less time to share. With less time devoted to building, the cultural preference for

Figure 10. Kisselburg House, ca. 1930 "pole" house, Cherokee County, N.C. (North Carolina Division of Archives and History, Western Office; photograph by the author).

small, replaceable dwellings was intensified. Many houses built during this era did not last the lifetime of their builders.

The building of log dwellings diminished considerably after the turn of the century. Individuals who continued to use log construction frequently built "pole" houses of small unhewn logs. Rather than continue building with logs or simply switching to frame, however, a large number of builders of small folk houses adopted a third method of construction. "Boxed" or "plank" construction provided a means of building small houses quickly and cheaply. Box construction differs from frame in that it has little internal framing. Instead, the vertical plank walls provide support for the structure. Although milled lumber was used, it was not cut to order. While rough planks bought from the sawmill were used to form the walls, the sills were often hand hewn and the house was roofed with hand split shingles or boards.[10]

Individuals who grew up during this era almost always distinguish between boxed and frame houses. Asked if they grew up in a frame or log house, several people responded, "No, it was plank [or boxed]." While some saw the distinction in terms of exterior appearance, many, especially men, also described plank houses as structurally different from frame. Robert Blanton described boxed houses in these terms: "Well back at that time, it meant, if you boxed it up and down. No insulation or nothing. Just one ply plank. No framing."[11] Similarly, Jim Neal and Bass Hyatt also characterized them as lacking framing: "Well you take a boxed house, take the boxed, they ain't got no framing in it. They just built the whole plate around and nail the boards down here up. And just slat it over. See a framed house, it got two by fours in it, put the weatherboarding on the outside like this and ceiling on the inside. Boxed house ain't got it."[12] "They'd nail the boxing down here at the sill and then up there to the plate. And that was all there was to it. Wasn't no framing in there."[13] On the other hand, a woman, Jessie Frazier, described boxed houses more in terms of the care that went into their construction: "Well it's when you, when they don't take no pains to cut the lumber all to pieces and fix it up fine. They just take planks and just set them up and nail them. You know, and just all around. Just kind of boxed 'em, we called boxing 'em in."[14]

Oral testimony indicates that boxed houses were extremely common in rural communities in southwestern North Carolina during the early twentieth century. Except for those who grew up in the river valleys, most individuals interviewed indicated that either log or boxed houses were the most common form of dwelling in their communities when they were children. The number of frame houses in many mountain communities could be counted on a single hand.

Houses of boxed construction were usually built by individuals who, a generation before, would have built a log home. They were often built by the owner with the help of family or neighbors. Unlike many rural

Figure 11. Front-gable boxed house. Ollie Fox House, ca. 1935, Jackson County, N.C. (North Carolina Division of Archives and History, Western Office; photograph by Rachel Barber).

frame houses of the early twentieth century, boxed houses followed the traditional plans of small folk houses, though they also reflected a growing preference for smaller and more numerous rooms. During the early twentieth century boxed and log houses were usually small. Frame houses were generally larger, less traditional in plan, and, unlike boxed houses, were often painted. Aesthetically, and as indicators of social status, log and boxed houses were generally viewed as equivalent.

By the 1930s, a new house type, based loosely on popular style, had made inroads into the average rural community. The changes represented by this stripped-down southern bungalow consisted primarily of the realigning of the roof line and the elimination of the fireplace. (Front-gabled houses, including the shotgun house, did not exist in the folk building repertoire of most rural southwestern North Carolinians.) These new houses were seldom much larger than the small traditional houses they replaced; three rooms were the average for both. Despite some similarities to traditional plan, however, the adoption of the front-gabled bungalow marked the final break from traditional plan in rural building in southwestern North Carolina.

Older people who reflect back usually see the 1940s as the decade when life really changed in their rural communities. After half a century of economic and social change, rural people found themselves living in a world that was quite different from that of their parents. Much of the region was no longer in local hands. Purchased first by speculators and timber interests, considerable portions of land subsequently came under control of the federal government through the creation of the Great Smoky Mountains National Park, the Tennessee Valley Authority, and national forest lands. While physical isolation continued to be a factor for some, family members were sent halfway across the world to fight in a world war.[15] Electricity finally began to come to even the remote communities. Although the region remained largely rural, agriculture alone could hardly be depended on to provide an adequate living for most families. Cooperative work practices and particularly building became mostly a memory. Stripped of their context, traditional buildings began to lose their meaning, except as artifacts and symbols of the past.

The visitor to rural southwestern North Carolina today might find the area complex and contradictory. Those fed on romantic images of southern Appalachia may be disappointed to discover that life progresses pretty much as it does elsewhere in the United States. People watch television, go to shopping malls, eat in fast-food chains. One needs to look beyond the surface, and the promotions of the local tourist industry, to find elements of traditional culture. When one does, the effect can be disquieting. Old English ballads, for example, are still passed down through oral tradition in a few families. While relatively rare, the continued survival of this tradition is remarkable.[16] Still, it is hard to celebrate, or even describe, these conservative elements of culture without some unease about contributing to the stereotypes that are often used to characterize the region.

Describing the cultural conservatism of southern Appalachia is problematic. But would it be right to deny those elements of culture that are conservative, such as the building of one-room log houses as late as the early twentieth century? One problem is that the conservative nature of Appalachian culture has not been set in the context of the conservatism of other regions and groups in rural America. To describe conservatism in Appalachian culture is not to imply that it is unique. Another problem is that conservatism has been equated with ignorance, the passive result of social and physical isolation. One might instead view cultural conservatism as an active, positive choice. Finally, conservatism is not monolithic. If a community actively conserves aspects of their tradition, it does not mean that other aspects are not open to change.

While elements of cultural conservatism remain, it is striking that despite the very conservative patterns of use during the early twentieth century, so little visible evidence remains of traditional spatial use, even in the homes of those who continue to live in old houses. In most dwellings little in the way of furnishing seems out of place with contemporary use. On occasion one does find beds in the living room, a pattern still acceptable to some older rural people, although sometimes medical reasons justify this seemingly traditional retention. One might also note a reluctance to fully utilize all available living space in some houses, *spatial usage* perhaps again connected to the retention of traditional spatial patterns, but also typical of older individuals who are living alone. One woman in Henderson County lived only in the rear ell of her mid-nineteenth-century I-house. This section was heavily renovated and comfortably furnished. The rest of the house was much like many old homeplaces, cared for but not inhabited. One of the few people I met who still lived in a log single pen house also confined his domestic space to the rear ell. The main section of the dwelling, the "big house," was used to store hay. Only in a few homes did one get a sense of past spatial use. The sitting room of Lolita Dean's turn-of-the-century saddlebag house was still furnished with a bed, chairs, and an organ as it had been in the early twentieth century. Letha Hicks still used a quilting frame suspended from the ceiling in her home in a remote section of Haywood County.

Some contemporary attitudes toward housing may reflect the impact of traditional viewpoints. The widespread acceptance of the mobile home is perhaps connected to the traditional ethic of building small, re-placeable dwellings. During the early twentieth century the acceptance of a single unbroken living space diminished as these spaces were carved into smaller and smaller portions while total living space often grew no larger. Perhaps the mobile home is a logical step in this progression. The total square feet of a mobile home is not substantially different from that of a typical single pen house, although the space has been carved up into a number of small rooms. The additions frequently appended to small houses may also reflect a traditional propensity for the incremen-tal building of houses in stages. Today even mobile homes often sprout front porches and additions off the rear.[17] Just as the cooperatively built log house provided some freedom from the cash economy, the mobile home may provide a freedom from the heavy indebtedness incurred by the purchase of a house. It is too easy to let prejudices and aesthetic judgments bias an understanding of the mobile home, just as in the past they prevented an objective view of the one-room "cabin." One must look beyond reasons of poverty to fully understand their acceptance.

Settlement patterns have remained relatively conservative although more than ever young adults leave their communities to find work and families tend to be much smaller. For most rural people, farming is a marginal occupation. Burley tobacco is one of the few crops that reaps a real profit; most farmers have nonfarming sources of income. Still, it is not uncommon for young adults, including some young professionals, to build a house and raise a family on land carved out of their parents' or grandparents' tract. Even those who have moved away are some-times given a parcel of land in case they wish someday to return. In keeping with tradition, new ranch houses and mobile homes encircle the bungalows and other dwellings built by the parents' generation in mid-century.

The traditional replaceability of dwellings was countered by the strong symbolic meaning ascribed to the homeplace. Attitudes of older rural people to the "old homeplace" give us access to the traditional meaning of the folk dwelling. Future studies might examine whether these attitudes survive among younger generations. Are the mobile homes and brick ranch houses destined to be the homeplaces for today's children? Or will traditional meanings go the way of traditional construction and spatial use?

This study, however, focuses on the past. In chapters 2 through 4 the relationship of traditional folk house forms to the social and symbolic use of these dwellings will be examined. In examining the single pen, double pen, and center-passage plans, these questions will be asked: Can the complexity of use be comprehended from a simple floor plan? How does the effect of social change on spatial use affect the physical form of the dwelling? And, how are the potential functional conflicts inherent in the dwelling resolved in physical form? Finally, chapter 5 will examine how the symbolic role of the homeplace affects the physical preservation or destruction of the house.

— major change; communal home building p. 30.

CHAPTER TWO

Big House: Use of the Single Pen Plan

Concentrating on words rather than structures brings into focus certain phrases that may be misunderstood or ignored during an architectural survey. One such phrase that emerged during this study was "big house." Kate Rogers of the Ellijay community in Macon County provided my first recorded usage of the term during the oral history phase of this study: "The [house] on the hill was more straight up. They had the kitchen, just the kitchen and the big house. . . . The beds went in the big house, and then, you sat in there too. It was all the fireplace and back here was all kinds of beds, and then there was the upstairs for beds."[1] During the course of subsequent interviews, it became apparent that this term was used by many older, rural people in southwestern North Carolina. Others, who did not actively use it, knew its meaning.

"Big house," used in reference to the architecture of the American South, usually conjures up images of antebellum plantations. In southwestern North Carolina, the term is applied, not to mansions, but to the smallest type in the regional repertoire of folk house forms, the single pen plan. "Big house" refers not as much to the specific house type, however, as to the concept of spatial use it embodies.

The single pen plan dwelling, so named by scholars, is often described as a one-room house. This definition is not altogether accurate. While the single pen house could be a one-room cabin, it often has two or three rooms and can have as many as five. (See Table 2.) Single unit is perhaps a better description of the way the plan was conceived, especially in log construction. The rectangular or square unit could be built one-and-a-half or two stories in height, creating an upstairs room. The downstairs of the rectangular single pen house could be partitioned, creating two rooms of unequal size on the bottom floor.

The most frequent addition to the single pen house was the separate kitchen. The kitchen was sometimes detached, and at times considerably removed from the house, or it was a rear shed or ell addition. Whether attached or detached, it was conceptually separate from the rest of the house. This plan was so common that "big house and kitchen" springs readily to the lips of those people who use the term "big house," including those who grew up in houses of less or more than two rooms. "A lot of folks called the living room and bedroom, the big house. You know, big house and the kitchen. You've heard the expression haven't you?" asked Addie Norton, although she grew up in a single pen house without a separate kitchen.[2] "Well, they, people back then called the living room, the big house. Big house and the kitchen," commented Eller Garrett, though she has known smaller and larger single pen houses during her life.[3] If the kitchen was in a functionally separate room, it was never part of the big house.

The various subplans possible among single pen houses account for some variety in the way the term "big house" is used. While the kitchen, if it existed, was not part of the big house, the upstairs or smaller room on the ground floor of the partitioned house may or may not be considered a part of the big house. Often an individual would define the big house as both the main dwelling unit (as opposed to the kitchen) and as the individual room where the majority of living took place. In an unpartitioned single pen house that is only one story in height, there would be no conflict in these two ways of using the term. However, in describing other variations of the plan, the use of "big house" could be seemingly contradictory. For instance, Mrs. Rogers described a dwelling as being "just the kitchen and big house," but later speaks of the

Table 2. Variations of the Single Pen Plan

Number of Rooms	Plan	Subvariations
One room	Big house	Square or rectangular
Two rooms	Big house and kitchen	Kitchen can be attached (rear ell or shed) or detached
	Big house and upstairs	One-and-a-half or full two stories in height
	Big house and back room (partitioned plan)	
Three rooms	Big house, kitchen, upstairs	One-and-a-half or two stories: kitchen can be attached or detached
	Big house, back room, and kitchen	Kitchen can be attached or detached
	Big house, back room, upstairs	One-and-a-half or full two stories
Four rooms	Big house, back room, upstairs, and kitchen	Kitchen can be attached or detached; height, one-and-a-half or full two stories
Five rooms	Big house, back room, upstairs, kitchen, and kitchen upstairs	Kitchen can be attached or detached; big house and kitchen can be either one-and-a-half or two stories

Figure 12. "Big house" with rear ell kitchen. F. W. Woody place, Cataloochee, N.C., in 1940 (Great Smoky Mountains National Park).

upstairs of that house as being separate from the big house.[4] Mary Jane Queen also implied that the upstairs was both part of and separate from the big house: "The big house, that's what we'd usually say. The big house and kitchen . . . that was the part, see, that you lived in, was what they call the big house. And then the kitchen. And then if you said upstairs, well, each one knew just exactly what you were talking about. If you meant the big house, kitchen or upstairs."[5]

In all these cases, big house refers to the room or physical unit where the majority of domestic activity took place. In rare instances, big house was used in reference to a larger house type. Again this term could be used to refer to the main dwelling unit or to the living room. The use of the term "big house" by descendants of well-to-do landholders to

Figure 13. Two-story single pen dwelling. Shadrick Guthrie House, ca. 1825, Buncombe County, N.C. (North Carolina Division of Archives and History, Western Office; photograph by Mary Jo Brezny).

describe the main unit of a large house may indicate the influence of lowland plantation society or some convergence of lowland and upland usage of the term.[6] On the other hand, the prevalent partitioning of single pen houses and the blurring of distinctions in spatial use of the single pen and double pen plans during the early twentieth century may have led to a broadening of the term simply to mean "living room."[7] The living room was also known as the "room we lived in," the "fireplace room," "the room with the hearth in it," or simply "the house." Still, the predominant use of the term "big house" in southwestern North Carolina continues to be in reference to the single pen dwellings.

One of the few academic references to the term is found in Hans Kurath's *Word Geography of the Eastern United States*: "In the simple

Figure 14. Partitioned single pen house with modern additions to the rear. Mull-Shields House, late nineteenth century, Cherokee County, N.C. (North Carolina Division of Archives and History, Western Office; photograph by the author).

homes of the piedmont and the mountains of North Carolina (also on the Peedee in South Carolina, rarely in West Virginia), the living room is called the big-house."[8] Kurath is essentially correct in the way that the term is used, but he does not attempt to account for its meaning. The big house was the living room, but usually only in cases where the majority of "living" took place in a single room.

Historical antecedents for the spatial preferences indicated by the term "big house" are easier to trace than the term itself. The spatial arrangements of late nineteenth- and early twentieth-century rural western North Carolinians were very similar to those of early New Englanders and common Englishmen during the sixteenth and seventeenth centuries.[9] The term "house" was sometimes used to refer to the living room or "hall" in both northern England and in New England during this time period.[10] M. W. Barley correlates this use of the term "house" in England to the continued existence of one-room dwellings.[11] The term "firehouse" was also used in England to denote a one-room cottage and, similar to the North Carolina "big house," it was sometimes used to mean the living room of a slightly larger house as well.[12] In late nineteenth- and early twentieth-century rural western North Carolina, "house" could refer to any living room, but "big house" generally had a more specialized meaning.

In the United States the term "big house" has been used to refer to the main dwelling unit in the southern plantation and in the New England connected farmhouse.[13] In both these cases "big" could simply refer to the physical size of the structure in comparison to the dependencies, but this interpretation makes less sense applied to the much smaller "big house" of the North Carolina mountains. Only one person interviewed, Arvel Greene, suggested that the house was "big" in comparison to the kitchen:

> They would build, when they got able, maybe first they would go and build just what was finally used as a kitchen and dining area. . . . And they managed though it was crowded, they managed to live in that for a period of time and with the expectation and looking forward to the time when they could build a big house. . . . That's why they spoke about going to the big house. Now that's the way it was in my learning and I don't know whether you have thought it that way or not.[14]

This explanation makes sense for those families who followed the pattern of first building a small cabin that later became the kitchen for a somewhat larger single pen house, but it is not adequate to explain the use of the term among families and communities where this was not the norm.[15] Nor does it adequately explain the various usages of the term, particularly in the cases where the big house did not have a separate kitchen.

Another possible linguistic antecedent may be the antiquated Scottish and northern English use of the word "big" as a verb meaning to live in or dwell.[16] The "big house" is indeed the room or structure in which one lives, a "dwelling house." (The word "house" was used for other structures that were not dwellings, such as smokehouses and springhouses.) This linguistic connection may be tenuous, but it is not inconceivable in a culturally conservative area such as rural western North Carolina where equally antiquated English and Scottish ballads are preserved by some families.

Although Old World antecedents have little meaning to current users of the term "big house," most think of the term as being old. "Just old-fashion talking," Zena Bennett put it, "a way of talking."[17] Asked why it was called the big house, Eller Garrett, among others, put her answer in the context of linguistic change: "Why did they call it the big house? I don't know; they'd say, 'it's in the big house' or 'go in and get me something in the big house.' . . . Now that's like they use to talk, you know. They'd start a revival in the fall, and nowadays they'll say they's 'going to a revival,' you know. And back then they'd say they was going to 'run a protracted meeting.' And why, you reckon? And they'd say 'meeting' and now they say 'go to church.' "[18] The important fact is that no one felt the term "big house" used in reference to houses that were quite small was either funny or odd. Although they now think of it as an old term, they also accept that it makes sense. As Monroe Ledford said, "I guess that's just the way people thought of it."[19]

To western North Carolinians, the big house was big because it was a relatively large undivided space. "It was a large, large room, usually accommodated two or three beds, double beds, plus chairs."[20] "It was a pretty big room. You know, it went from there, way back here. You know, it was a great big room. And I don't know, I believe us young'uns would call it the big house."[21] It was conceptually big not only because it consisted of a large unbroken space, but because of the many functions unified within it. It was a room for socializing and household chores, for sleeping and sitting, and for many people it was also a room

Figure 15. Making baskets in front of the hearth (John C. Campbell Folk School).

for cooking and eating. "Big house" is primarily associated, however, with its function as the center of family and social activity. In answer to the question "what was the big house?," Letha Hicks recalled, "That's where they stayed I reckon. Where they, you know, when they come in from work. Set and talked and worked. They come in of a evening, sit and scrape splits. Through the wintertime, now, is when they done that. Made them chairs. My mom and pap worked on them."[22] Mary Messer remembered, "It's where we stayed, you know, most of the time. We called it the big house, where we had company you know. I wouldn't know any other way."[23] Mary Jane Queen also associated the big house with socializing: "That was the main living area if, if you said the big

Big house for socializing

house, then that was where we all gathered at any time when, like what I was saying these parties or anything, we all went into the big house." [24]

Understanding the big house is important, not because the term is an example of antiquated language use but because the big house represents a system of organizing and appreciating space. Of all aspects of social and symbolic use of folk houses in southwestern North Carolina, it is this organization of space that differs the most from contemporary mainstream architectural use. Why did people choose the big house and the system of spatial use it embodied? Clearly for many western Carolinians, it was a choice. While the pioneer conditions of the early settlement days or the poverty of the region in later years may have been motivating factors in this choice, it is evident that the plan was not chosen solely by force of necessity.

The one-room cabin was, of course, a popular pioneer house form. Some people did build them only as temporary homes until they had the time and money to build larger houses. Many western North Carolinians, however, replaced small cabins with slightly larger single pen houses. The house form itself persisted throughout the nineteenth and into the twentieth century, long after true pioneer conditions had vanished. Although the rural elites did build larger homes, not all builders of single pen houses were poor or uneducated. Many, if not cash rich, were owners of substantial plots of land. As Zena Bennett noted, "People use to, they didn't count rich in money then, they count rich in land and property." [25] While increased access to milled lumber did make it easier to build frame houses, the continued use of log construction was not restricted only to isolated mountain communities. For instance, around 1896 Jack Drake built his single pen log house barely a few miles outside of Hendersonville, then (and now) one of the largest towns in southwestern North Carolina. Drake, who became sheriff of Henderson County, later built a frame house on the same piece of property.

Objectively, economic conditions in Appalachia during the late nineteenth and early twentieth centuries were well below the national stan-

Figure 16. Jack Drake House. Single pen log dwelling, ca. 1896, Henderson County, N.C. (North Carolina Division of Archives and History, Western Office; photograph by the author).

dard. However, there is nothing to indicate that everyone who lived in single pen houses could not afford an alternative. Most small folk houses were built cooperatively, with little cash outlay. Small dwellings were considered movable and replaceable. Old houses were abandoned and new ones built. One family was reported to have switched alternately between two single pen log houses on the same property. "Well you get tired of one place and you go to the other. One of them it was about half a mile up the creek from that. We had about three hundred acres. We just went from one to the other until we built the one standing there now," Robert Blanton recalled.[26]

The pattern of routine abandonment and replacement and the cooperative nature of building in this region suggest that larger houses could have been built by more people if it had been a cultural priority. If people could afford to own several houses on their property or easily replace the ones they lived in, the cooperative building system could have provided larger houses for little cash outlay. However, the cooperative nature of the building system reinforced the continued building of small folk houses. If people wanted something substantially different from their neighbors, they had to pay for labor. The early twentieth century did bring a growing preference for more rooms although the economic situation was generally not improving for most rural people in southwestern North Carolina. It was not that people could suddenly afford more rooms, but that they wanted them and therefore built them. The people who grew up in single pen houses do not say "we could not afford a bigger house," they say "we didn't know anything else." Of course, most were aware of the existence of larger houses, but their family and community intimately "knew" the organization of space and patterns of living within the single pen house.

Conditions within single pen houses varied considerably. The plan could house a single individual or a family of twelve. Some single pen houses were well built and finely finished; in others people "lived on the dirt."[27] "One room and no floor in it. I don't know how she lived," a man commented about a poor neighbor's house.[28] The single pen house could also vary in size substantially. Some houses were small and square while others were "built long," a term used to describe the larger rectangular versions of the plan. Eller Garrett described the houses she lived in when she first married as "little pens," but her grandparents' "real huge" house was also just one room.[29] Size or quality of the house was not necessarily judged by the number of rooms. Poor people lived in single pen houses but so did some folks "rich in land and property."

Rich or poor, the choice to live in a single pen house involved accepting a complex system of spatial use. Oral testimony illuminates those complexities that cannot be read from the plan alone. The descriptions of life within the big house by those who experienced it demonstrate that the simple house form belies the nature of the spatial system it encompassed.

Within the single pen plan house a large "all purpose" room takes the place of many rooms with specialized functions, therefore suggesting generalized room use. In describing the room use as generalized, however, it would be wrong to assume that specific functions were not assigned to individual spaces. Oral testimony indicates that although physical space was not architecturally divided into discrete units, it was indeed divided, physically and conceptually, for practical, social, and symbolic purposes. For instance, architectural evidence may not always reveal the physical barriers used to partition a room. Light board partitions were common, but some people simply used a curtain or blankets. Recalling her childhood home, Addie Norton recalled that it "was just one big room. And we curtained it off, made two rooms. Bedroom for two beds in the back and in the living room, we had the kitchen and the living room and everything together. Just a little log house, now that's what I was borned in and raised in."[30] Those who did not visually partition a room still used physical means to divide up space. Beds, as the largest and often the most common pieces of furniture, frequently served this purpose. Kate Rogers spoke of one such division: "[Uncle Jack Moore's house] was built long. And the middle here was just like a hall but it wasn't a hall. They had a bed on one side and a bed on the other side all the way back. . . . It wasn't laid out in rooms. It was just beds, a bed here and a bed there, you see." And later in the interview: "[There were] different styles of houses. Some of them you know, like I told you about, a hallway, not a hallway, just a walkway between the beds."[31]

Conceptually, the single room was divided into specialized places. This was particularly necessary when there was no separate kitchen. Sleeping tended to be isolated on one end of the room while cooking, eating, and sitting focused around the other end. Several individuals described this arrangement of spatial use: "We had three [beds] across the back of it. It was about, I don't know, I think it was twenty by, I don't remember. But there was plenty of room for three beds. And then all the front of it was then, we'd sit around the fire and there was a table and a stove" (Essie Moore).[32] "But the big house at Grandma's, it was a great big house and in the front room was, there was two beds back

Figure 17. The hearth was the heart of the house. Interior of Bumgarner big cabin, Deep Creek, N.C., in 1937 (Great Smoky Mountains National Park).

there at the back and up front, the kitchen: the stove, the table, and still there was room for them all to get around the fire" (Kate Rogers).[33] "I've been in log houses, they'd have the beds in the back of the house, in the back of the room, and up at the front have their table, and they'd have their pots and their pans and cooked on the fire most of them, and then they, maybe they had a little stove over in the corner they'd cook on, and then on the other side they'd have the water buckets and things like that. And they lived, and had plenty. Lived to be old" (Lolita Dean).[34] In all these descriptions, the front and back of the house are oriented to the hearth, not to the front door. The hearth was indeed the heart of the house, and a place for sitting around the hearth was an essential element of this spatial arrangement.

Until the twentieth century many people who lived in single pen houses cooked on the open hearth. Those who acquired cook stoves tended to build a separate kitchen to house them. Some, however, in-stalled the stove in the big house but still preserved the open hearth. "Sometimes now they didn't ever get that kitchen built for the cook stove, it set maybe right in the corner beside the fireplace."[35] Cooking and eating took place to one side of the hearth and sitting to the other. "But there was plenty of room, they sat over here on this side, most everybody did, and you cooked on the other."[36] The kitchen tended to be conceptually separate even when it was located within the big house; a room within a room. As Mrs. Rogers explained: "When we moved down there though, there wasn't any partitions down below. The chimney, the big house, be all there was. We had the kitchen in one corner."[37]

When the kitchen was removed from the big house, the use of space was more fluid. Depending on need, beds were more evenly distributed around the room. The chimney corners were popular locations for beds; still, enough room was always allowed around the hearth for family and social activities. Memories of family life are therefore frequently tied to the hearth, the social and symbolic center of the household. "[Mother would] sing Rock of Ages, Lord Thomas, oh, lots of different songs. Pappy, he'd help her. We'd sit in the chimney corner, us little ones would. They'd get in front and they'd sit there and chew their tobacco and sing, and spit in the fire. And she was a real singer, too" (Letha Hicks).[38]

The functional divisions of the big house were temporal as well as spatial. Although beds usually dominated the space of the big house, the room was not thought of as a bedroom. During the day, the social functions of the big house predominated; only at night did it become a sleeping room. This flexibility provided an efficient use of small space, as different functions dominated during different times of day.

Functional use of space was divided temporally not only by night and day, but also by the seasons of the year. The use of the big house was more complex during the winter when more activities were confined to the inside of the dwelling. During the other months, the tasks re-quired of farm life kept many family members out of the big house for the majority of the day. Several women remembered that as children

Figure 18. Beds dominated the space of the big house. Mattress airing on porch of Will Harmon log cabin, Cades Cove, Tenn., in 1936 (Great Smoky Mountains National Park).

they preferred farm work to being cooped up inside with household chores. Household activity, however, could also be moved outside during warmer months; a number of people remember sewing and weaving taking place on the porch. The porch or yard also absorbed a good deal of social activity when the weather was mild.

The single pen house was also adapted to needs of the social life of the community. The nature of social activity varied considerably among families and communities. Although not all approved of dancing, some communities held dances regularly. As community buildings were generally limited to churches and schools in rural western North Carolina, dances were often held in people's homes. Beds and other furniture were removed from the room, and the big house became a room for dancing.

Figure 19. Kitchen separated from the big house by roofed walkway. Ephraim Bumgarner cabins, Deep Creek, N.C., in 1937 (Great Smoky Mountains National Park).

In a single pen house it may be assumed that the use of space is collective, as well as generalized. People add rooms to a house either to separate functions or to separate people. As we have seen, however, space needs to be functionally divided even in houses which are not partitioned into discrete rooms. It is also apparent that if there was no individualization of space within the big house, life would have been intolerable. Beds constituted the largest area of individualized space. In Kate Rogers's childhood home, a bed was placed in every corner of the house, upstairs and downstairs, except the corner where the staircase was located. As she said, "everybody knowed his corner." In Mrs. Rogers's family, as in many others, the status of the head of household or eldest member was indicated by the position of the bed near the hearth. Her father's bed occupied one chimney corner, and when her grandmother moved in with the family, she was given the other. "The house was so big and that big chimney, there's room for her bed on the side up there by the fire."[39] Parents and grandparents would also have their specific place to sit in front of the hearth while children often sat on the floor or on makeshift seats to the side. If visual privacy was seldom achieved in the big house, individuals had and knew their own space.

Young children, of course, were allotted the least individual space. Several children often shared a single bed, with one child sometimes relegated to the foot. But even children sometimes felt the need to assert their own space: "Big house and kitchen. That was all you ever hear them mention. Never hear them mention the bedrooms. They mention their bed though. 'Now my bed, now there ain't nobody come in here, put me out of my bed and me have to sleep at the foot of mama's bed or on a pallet,' you'd hear them say that." Though, of course, children were frequently turned out of their beds for company, and as Mrs. Rogers hastened to add, "it was nice to sleep even on a pallet in front of that big fireplace, in the winter."[40]

The increasing desire for individualized architectural space has been equated with the growth of individualism in modern society.[41] The traditional Appalachian community, however, did not repress all individuality. If one wanted to benefit from the community one had to conform to certain norms, but within those confines a degree of individuality was achieved. In a similar manner, individual space was acquired within the confines of the big house. Individuality and individual space were not given, but they could be achieved.

To a person who has never experienced a single pen house, the biggest drawback to the plan would seem to be crowding and the lack of privacy. Conditions in some houses were extremely crowded, at least by modern standards:

> Now here in this [former one-room log house], I heard my father, I wasn't born yet, I heard him tell about when he was just a boy. There was, he was staying with these folks by the

name of Moody. And they raised eight girls, no boys in their family, in this little old room and up there [upstairs]. But they finally built a little lean-to right there where they had a cook stove and a cook table through that door right there. And so, the man needed some man or boy to help him lots, things maybe girls didn't do. And so, they had my father stay with them five years before he was married, he stayed here. And there was Mr. and Mrs. Moody and their eight girls and my father lived in this. (Arvel Greene)[42]

There's lot of people back in those days, raised big families in one-room log houses. There's a log house standing up there on Skeenah now that's very little bigger than this living room. And there was a family with five boys reared up in that house. It had a little, narrow, steps up in the corner of it, almost straight up. But, the room over the upstairs, was as big as the bottom room and I guess they had three or four beds up there maybe. I don't know maybe more. But that was my dad's aunt and he's told me about staying there with his cousins many a night, you know. So, not only the family lived in that little house, but they took care of their company, too. (Monroe Ledford)[43]

People who grew up in single pen houses, however, seldom complain about either crowding or lack of privacy.[44] Instead they assert that everyone lived the same way and they "didn't know anything else." Arvel Greene noted, "We didn't have room for nothing hardly, but we didn't get hot under the collar and worry and fret much about it because we were still just born and growed up that way. We just didn't need, or no use to want, for more room."[45] "Now when we were coming up, two or three of us boys were sleeping together, and that was just fine, we didn't pay any attention. Now, people don't like, they want one room to themselves. Everybody to themselves. But back then we didn't know no different, see we didn't pay no attention to it," Grady Carringer similarly recollected.[46]

There is little evidence that the small house caused undue tension within the family. Some even felt they got along better then. Asked if people felt crowded in one-room houses, one woman responded, "They got along better than they do nowadays. They just, well there wasn't many people any better off. They about all lived the same back then." [47] If there were family tensions, the house plan was usually not blamed. As Robert Blanton, one of ten children, joked: "The house was all right, but we'd fight all the time anyway." [48]

The acceptance of what seems to be a high level of crowding does not necessarily indicate a disregard for personal privacy. Notions of what constitutes privacy vary considerably. Today many people would be shocked at the idea of adults sleeping in the same room, not only with their children but also with parents or in-laws, although it was an accepted norm for many western North Carolinians. (Generally priority was given to separating older children from adults, rather than separating various generations of adults.) When several adults did sleep in the same room, some degree of privacy could be achieved through the arrangement of the beds. As Zena Bennett explained:

> Well now Granny White's over there, they, talk about a big house, they did. They had, oh they had a big farm, pretty farm and raised everything. They had a kitchen built off too. And they had a big, living, big house, they called it a big house. They had about six beds in that one room. But they had those big old high post beds, and the way they could turn every bed, why you got to bed, nobody else couldn't see you behind the bed. Now that's the way they do it, now that's the truth.[49]

This privacy was of a limited nature, but it demonstrates that, rather than disregard the notion, people made efforts to create privacy when possible. Without walls to hide behind, individuals had to exercise care in their relationships with others in the house. Willa Mae Pressley, who felt that she was raised to be a private person, commented, "I think they really did [respect privacy], but they just went about it in different ways from the way you do now. Yes, you respected people's privacy." [50]

The small house not only had to encompass the family, which on an average was large, but also a generally high level of sociability. As Monroe Ledford said, "Not only the family lived in that little house, but they took care of their company, too."[51] Many families not only regularly fed or entertained guests, they also put them up overnight. Adolescents, in particular, participated in routine visiting: "Us boys, we never did like to work on Saturday. You know, we'd work through the week. So, if the other boys didn't come in pretty quick to spend the night with us, we wanted to go and spend the night with them," remembered Gilford Williams.[52] Girls too participated in routine visiting, as Zena Bennett recalled. "Lots of people spend the night. Then us girls we always, on weekends, go somewhere spend the night or let them come, we'd have visitors. Go back and forth, that's the way we did. Why we didn't never get lonesome." Later she added, "Boys them days be a courting, lots of them lived far off. They'd spend the night, and eat supper and breakfast."[53] Room would always be made to accommodate visitors. Children would double up in beds, and pallets would be made upon the floor.

It was part of the ethic of many families to welcome strangers as well as friends, to offer them food and a place to sleep. Often this ethic held even in the face of perceived danger. Anna Collett's family often had visitors due to the location of their house on a mountain road between the towns of Andrews and Franklin. One of her narratives tells of a suspicious stranger:

> And another thing that happened, is a man.
>
> When mom and dad'd go to milk, me and Herman, that's my brother, him and me have to get in wood and kindling for morning to make fires. And so we got our wood in, and we's setting in front of the fireplace, whittling on some little old things. We'd float these things we'd make on the water.
>
> Somebody knocked on the door. And my brother said, "Come in if your nose is clean." They knocked again. He said, "Scratch under."
>
> Nobody came in.
>
> I said, "Herman, you better not say that no more."

We'd always tease one another and knock at the door, some of us come answer the door, and it'd be one of us.

I said, "That might not be one of the young'uns." I said, "That might be someone else." And he said, "You go see."

So I got up and went to the door, and there stood a man.

And I spoke to him and he said, "Where's your daddy?" And I said, "He's at the barn amilking." "Well," he said, "I'd like to stay all the night." I said, "You go out to the barn and see him."

So he went on out there and asked daddy if he could stay all night and they told him yes. So they come on back to the house and me and Herman we cleaned up our mess we had in front of the fire.

And so, Daddy ask him if he had any supper and he said no. So Mama set out what was left from our supper on the table. And he'd eaten, he said he'd like to go to bed.

So we put him upstairs. Daddy thought he acted suspicious. And we put him upstairs to sleep. (One of the older young'uns was gone then.) And we fastened the door from the downstairs until he couldn't get back down.

So the next morning he got up. Daddy called up the stairs and told him to come down, breakfast was ready. He come down and eat.

And, then he went off walking. And he hadn't been gone but about an hour 'til the law come and ask us, described the man.

Daddy told them, yes, he spent the night. He said, "Well which way did he go?" And Daddy told him.

And he went down below our house 'bout a mile there was an old barn. And they found him in that barn.

He'd killed a man and had run away. And there he was staying in our house.

The Lord took care of us.

The family did take the precaution of putting the man upstairs, so they could latch the door, a violation of the norm of having adults sleep downstairs. However, they did not question their duty to take in the stranger. Neither potential threat nor the dubious morals of a stranger prevented the family from fulfilling this obligation. In another of Anna Collett's stories, a young woman and an older man, claiming to be married, were permitted to spend the night. They, too, were hauled off by the law in the morning.[54]

While the Colletts had a larger double pen house, the welcoming of friends and strangers to spend the night was also common among those who lived in single pen dwellings. In this way people overcame the hardships of traveling in a mountainous area as well as the social limitations of geographic isolation. Room would be made to accommodate visitors whatever the size of the house.

By modern standards the single pen house would seem to make the achievement of privacy difficult not just for the individual but also for the family unit. The single pen plan is the most extreme of those house types that have been characterized as "socially open." Entering through the front door, the non-family member gains access to the heart of family activity. In the single pen plan this access is extended as the majority of domestic activity is encompassed within the single room entered. It is important to note, however, that traditionally the family unit inhabiting the single pen house had relatively little need to protect their private sphere. The rural community in southwestern North Carolina was traditionally an extended family, metaphorically and quite often literally. Until the early twentieth century, the average single pen dweller worked in the private realm of the family farm, interacting primarily with family members and neighbors. With the immediate world outside the house not so clearly distinguished from the family unit dwelling inside the walls of the house, the privacy of the family unit was not apt to be so assiduously protected.[55]

The sense of the community as extended family began to erode as more and more individuals were drawn into "public" work outside the home. Early additions and alterations to the single pen plan tended to enhance the privacy of the family unit rather than that of its individual members. During the early twentieth century cooking, eating, and eventually sleeping were moved out of the room immediately accessible to outsiders. In many families the accepted norm of sleeping in the same room with one's children or one's in-laws survived much longer than the tradition of cooking in the main room. When asked about crowding one woman commented not on the fact that she and her husband slept in the same room with her mother-in-law but that "If people come you'd feel crowded, and my mother-in-law didn't mind. She had a lot of things she cooked on the fireplace and had hooks you know and things that way, she didn't mind it. But it aggravated me to think anybody's watching me. And she said the preachers use to come and sit around the fire too, and she had to do her cooking before them."[56]

The concept of privacy is multifaceted and may include intimacy as well as solitude.[57] Aloneness was difficult to find within the single pen though certainly not in the forests and agricultural lands that surrounded the home. Individual and conjugal privacy were not totally disregarded; non-architectural means (the arrangement of beds or the use of blanket partitions) and perhaps more important, non-physical means, such as the cultivation of reserve and a sense of respect, protected individuals from some unnecessary intrusions. Privacy, though not solitude, was also achieved through the intimacy of the family. Compared to other house plans the single pen house only minimally protected the privacy of the domestic unit, but rather than be threatened by it, the intimacy of the family extended outward from the home to encompass the rural community. In the days before the majority of community members were drawn into public work, the relative solitude of agricultural work and the isolation of the rural community led in fact to the cultivation of sociability. The need for a social life outweighed the pressures of crowding in the small folk house, as the frequency of visiting and the housing of strangers attests. In the nineteenth century those neighbors who desired larger houses added public spaces rather than private spaces to their houses.[58]

These various testimonies indicate that those who lived in single pen houses shared a system of spatial use in that they

held common ideas about the use of domestic space: how it is to be functionally divided or allotted to individuals and what barriers people de-
mand to have between themselves and others. However, there was also
considerable variation in how these houses were specifically furnished
and arranged. These variations were due to differences in the size and
economic status of families, the possible alternative room layouts with
the single pen house type and the gradual changes in spatial preferences
that occurred in the late nineteenth and early twentieth centuries.

Differences in furnishing tended to reflect economic distinctions
rather than profound differences in spatial use. For many families the
furniture was minimal; a bed or beds of some form, a few straight-back
chairs, and a table were generally the essentials in the one-room house.
Eller Garrett described the first house she lived in after she married:
"We lived in that little tiny house. We had one bed in it and our table.
And three or four chairs. And I had a box nailed up in the back of the
house to put our clothes in. What few we had."[59] Addie Norton's childhood home had little more: "Mostly just beds, we didn't have room to
put anything. We had straight chairs, homemade chairs, we didn't have
a rocker or anything. . . . Stove and the dining table and the chairs about
took it up, you know."[60] Arvel Greene described in detail the home he
lived in when he was young:

> Well, we really just had one room. It was built a small cabin,
> one room, except we finally partitioned off a part of that room
> and made one little bitty tiny bedroom where you could put a
> bed in it. Then we had what we called a lean-to kitchen and
> dining room. It was just a little shed off the back side of the
> house. And, in that, we had an old wood stove, a cook stove,
> a small one, and a cook table, a kitchen table to do the work
> on and then right in the other end of it, kind of, we had sort of
> you'd call it a dining room, or a dining table. And we had an
> old mud and rock fireplace for heat in the side of the big room.
> So that was kind of a small layout.[61]

Although some houses were small, the furnishings were not necessarily poor. Monroe Ledford described the furnishings in his grandparents' single pen house in this manner: ". . . two beds in it. And a table, two tables, and chairs, and a cherry cupboard they called it. One of the finest pieces of furniture, it'd bring a pile of money now." [62]

The average size of single pen houses varied across different communities. The story-and-a-half one-room house was common in some communities and apparently rare in others. People in some single-story houses only had a "loft" big enough to accommodate storage. "Wasn't tall up there, but they could put a lot of old junk up there in the loft. Lay up things. They had to lay up things sometimes to keep us young'uns from getting it" (Letha Hicks). [63] The story-and-a-half house generally had an "upstairs" that was almost always the domain of the older children. Parents, babies, and sometimes grandparents would sleep on the first floor. In many cases the upstairs was accessible only by a ladder. Mary Jane Queen retained a vivid memory of the house she lived in until she was five years old, a story-and-a-half log house without a separate kitchen:

> And they had beds, let's see three beds. They had a bed downstairs, I mean on the first floor and the others was upstairs for the children. But it was, it was not a real small house, nor it wasn't too big. But it would be enough that we had a stove and a fireplace and then room for a bed and chairs. . . . Fireplace was like over here, stove was back here. See, and then the bed was here and over there was where we would go up and down the ladder into this upstairs part. And then, of course we had chairs. It was, oh, a whole lot bigger than that living room in there. You know the first floor and the upstairs was the same size. [64]

During the early twentieth century the story-and-a-half single pen house became less common as box construction superseded log as the preferred building technique for small folk houses. Builders of boxed houses who wanted more room tended to spread laterally in their construction; most did not build over a story in height.

Throughout the nineteenth century, it is probable that some single pen houses were partitioned on the first floor. As many others were subsequently partitioned in the late nineteenth and early twentieth centuries, it is difficult to judge the frequency of this arrangement prior to that time.[65] Both Monroe Ledford and Kate Rogers described partitioned single pen houses without separate kitchens belonging to their grandparents. Mrs. Rogers described her grandparents' house as "partitioned off, but the kitchen and the big room, the big house, was together." Cooking was done on a small stove located next to the fireplace, while at Mr. Ledford's grandparents', cooking was done on the hearth.[66]

The smaller room of the partitioned single pen house was usually quite small, containing little more than one or more beds. People called this small room by several different names. Some refer to the smaller room as a bedroom, though this term may be retrospectively applied due to its function; others denied that the word bedroom was ever used. For some it was simply "the other room." During the early twentieth century, as the term "front room" (applied to the former big house) grew in popularity, the designation "back room" was sometimes used. (Again, "front" and "back" are oriented to the hearth rather than the front door.) A few combined old and new terminology. "The big house is what they call the home, the big house. And then the kitchen. And the back room. Those the three names they had. Back room, kitchen, and big house" (Letha Hicks).[67]

A kitchen, separate from the big house, was also a possibility throughout the nineteenth century, though similar to the partitioned first floor, it became more common during the late nineteenth and early twentieth centuries. Many of the older kitchens were completely separate units with their own hearths, set at a distance away from the house. A few were older family homes that had been replaced as the main dwelling unit by a larger single pen house, but generally, people had few explana-

[handwritten margin note: Evolution of terms as the house grew in size]

tions for the placement of the kitchen some distance from the dwelling. As ninety-two-year-old Larry Gunter mused, "But my grandfather, I never could understand why he built that large kitchen away from his big house."[68] Only one person mentioned a fire hazard[69] and another scoffed at the idea, "They had the chimney in the house where they slept, and it was the one that had the fire in it."[70]

The kitchen, when separate from the house, was relegated to the status of outbuilding. It served a specialized function and did not have the complex overlay of practical and social uses associated with the house. Though sleeping might be packed into all other available spaces, the kitchen was seldom used for this purpose.[71] By the late nineteenth century, kitchens were generally built closer to the house, though many country carpenters continued to keep them physically separate. A space of several feet might be left between the big house and the kitchen, or, even if the buildings adjoined, an interior door was not always cut between the rooms. One had to step outside to enter the kitchen. As common as this "long-handed practice" was, few people had a "practical" reason for the lack of an interior door.[72] A few mentioned the scarcity of interior space, though this makes sense only if a back door leading from the living room outside was also seen as a necessity.[73] If both the kitchen and the big house were of log, it was easiest to build them as separate units with the double-thick log wall between the two rooms making the framing of a doorway difficult. However, many added kitchens were of boxed or frame construction, and even larger frame houses sometimes lack an interior doorway between the living room and kitchen.

The growing preference for a separate kitchen during the late nineteenth and early twentieth centuries can be associated with the growing specialization of room use. There was, however, also a more practical impetus. For many families the addition of a kitchen was directly linked to the acquisition of a cook stove. Stoves were thought of in terms of cooking and not heating, and it is a testament to the social and symbolic significance of the hearth that for many decades few people thought to replace the open hearth with a stove. Some people crowded the stove

Purposive building

in the corner next to the hearth, but the majority found it more practical to build a separate room for it. Although the open hearth was not immediately abandoned, stoves brought radical changes to the domestic habits of rural people in southwestern North Carolina. Significantly, a large number of people remember the exact model of their family's stove, and those whose families acquired a stove after they were born often have vivid memories of the event. Tiny Arms remembers going to fetch the family's first stove:

> I might have been eight or nine or ten years old. It was a second-handed stove. Aunt Lily Davis bought her one of the first range stoves come in, and she let mother have it. And I took a yoke of oxens and a sled and went and got it. Yeah, and I passed some of the boys down on the hill and they just hollered and laughed at me, I was driving those steers. Lord, they were just as gentle as they could be, they weren't no trouble. So I took those steers and sled and went and got that stove.[74]

The separate kitchen satisfied both conservative and progressive cultural trends. The cook stove eased domestic burdens, and building a kitchen to house it eased the crowding in the big house and separated the function of cooking away from the house. However, the separate kitchen also preserved the sanctity of the hearth in the big house by removing the usurping stove to a separate room. Dining usually followed cooking into the addition.

The removal of the kitchen from the big house was cause, as well as result, of a preference for separating cooking and eating from social activities around the hearth. Separated for the convenience of the cook stove, the new kitchen arrangement brought a preference for functional separation to a new generation. As Bessie Tilley mentioned, she disliked the idea of cooking in front of people, though her mother-in-law did not mind it.[75] Many people reported that even after the acquisition of a cook stove, their grandmothers or mothers preferred to cook certain items on the hearth. Cornbread in particular was said to have tasted

~~just like beer out of a bottle !~~

better when cooked at the fireplace. It is also possible that women of the older generation enjoyed the ritual or social aspects of cooking within the center of family activity.

The majority of kitchens constructed after the acquisition of the stove were built either as a shed or ell addition. Unlike earlier kitchens, they usually lacked a fireplace. Although a number of people remember totally detached kitchens, none remember any being built. However, Berzilla Wallin recalls that when her family acquired their first stove, her mother's loom house was converted to a kitchen.[76] This conversion made perfect sense, for as domestic patterns changed due to the availability of certain consumer goods in mountain communities, both handweaving and cooking on the hearth rapidly declined. Those who remember weaving recall that separate outbuildings or an enclosed porch were usually used to house the loom. Spinning continued as a domestic activity in many households long after weaving and was always associated with the hearth.

During the late nineteenth and early twentieth centuries, three-room arrangements were probably the most common variants of the single pen house. These would consist either of an "upstairs," "big house," and "kitchen" or a "front room," "back room," and "kitchen." The latter arrangement, built as a unit with a rear shed kitchen, was one of the most common types of boxed houses built during the early twentieth century. Although these are sometimes classified as "hall and parlor" plan houses, they are more directly related to the single pen plan. An identical arrangement is created by partitioning and adding on to a one-room log house. Without a hearth, the bedroom or back room lacked the complex overlay of formal and private functions associated with traditional use of the parlor.[77] If the house did not have an upstairs, as was common for many boxed houses, the bedroom was where the older children slept. Until several decades into the twentieth century, the parents in many families continued to sleep in the room with the hearth.[78] The first family home remembered by Minnie McDonald, a boxed or plank house, followed this pattern: "Well my mother and daddy had a bed in that room with a fireplace in it. And then they had three beds in another room where all of us slept. Then they had the kitchen and dining room together." The youngest child slept with the parents.[79]

During the late nineteenth century there was some degree of room specialization and individualization of space manifested within the single pen plan itself. Cooking and eating were increasingly isolated from the functions of the big house. Some effort was made to segregate adults and children in sleeping arrangements. Still, the "big house" existed in concept. People still "lived" in one room, overlaid in functions. The upstairs and back room were peripheral, the realm of children; and the kitchen was given the status of an outbuilding. Functionally, the big house still served as the parents' bedroom, the least private but warmest place in the house, and the open hearth remained both the main source of heat and the social center of the house.

The rejection of traditional spatial patterns came at different times, varying according to specific family or rural community. A person born as late as the 1930s may describe many elements of traditional patterns of spatial use in their family.[80] By that time other families had rejected them completely. The term "big house" itself began to pass out of active use. Vestal Cochran's family built a new house after the first one burned when she was nine (during World War I). The first house had a "big house," the second did not.[81]

Individuals who thought of themselves as progressive stopped viewing the term as proper. "We use to use it way back yonder. We don't, I never did use it much. . . . I always called the rooms by their right names as near as possible."[82] The term passed so quickly out of active usage that people under the age of sixty often do not know its meaning.

The trend was not only toward more rooms, it was also toward smaller spaces. Though they tended to follow traditional plans, boxed houses usually had smaller rooms than log houses. The large unbroken spaces of older houses were frequently "cut down" (partitioned). Either in building new houses or altering old ones, many rural people ended up with no more room, just more rooms.

Even those who spoke most approvingly of old houses expressed the growing preference for smaller rooms that developed during their life-times. Zena Bennett, speaking of Granny White's big house after it passed to the next generation, commented, "They had it all cut down. . . . They made a nice place out of it." [83] As a schoolgirl, Kate Rogers left her family's log single pen house to board with a family who had a new plank house. "It was really built nice, just roomy and everything was cut to itself," she said.[84] Oma Jenkins expressed the disapproval she had felt of the house her sister and brother-in-law built, "It was a big house, but they didn't cut it up enough rooms." [85]

At first extra rooms were simply attached to the basic single pen plan, and many houses still focused on a single hearth. By the 1920s and 1930s, however, traditional plans and the hearth itself disappeared in new construction, though many rural people continued to live in old houses. Spatial behavior within older houses also began to change. Many no longer saw the living room as the proper place for beds. The heads of household retreated to private bedrooms, and more rooms were provided for the children, either through the partitioning of space within the house or through additions. The idea of the "big house" had disappeared, except in the memories of those people who knew its meaning.

There is no absolute means of determining the prevalence of the single pen house in rural southwestern North Carolina during the nineteenth and early twentieth centuries. These small traditional houses are the least likely to survive on the landscape today. Although no argument can be made for its statistical significance, it should be noted that over two-thirds of the individuals interviewed lived in a single pen house at some point in their lives. (See Table 3.) For some it was just a vague memory of an early childhood home (which was soon replaced by a larger dwelling) or it was the house to which the person first "went to housekeeping." [86] For others, it was a more permanent home. Several individuals who had never lived in a version of this house type spoke of relatives or neighbors who had.

Many today would like to deny the prevalence of the house type, see-ing it as a negative stereotype of southern Appalachia. Of course, there

Table 3. Types of Folk Houses Lived in by Informants

Informants Grouped by Year of Birth	Single Pen	Double Pen	Center-Passage Traditional	Center-Passage Nontraditional
1881–85				
1	x			
1886–90				
1	x			
2	x		x	
1891–95				
1	x	x		
2	x			
3	x	x		
4	x			
5	x	x		
6	x			
1896–1900				
1	x			
2	x			
3	x	x	x	
4			x	
5		x		
6	x		x	
7			x	
8		x		
9		x	x	
1901–5				
1	x			x
2	x	x		
3		x		
4		x		
1906–10				
1		x		
2		x	x	
3		x		
4	x	x		
5	x			
6		x		x

Table 3 (continued)

Informants Grouped by Year of Birth	Single Pen	Double Pen	Center-Passage Traditional	Center-Passage Nontraditional
7		x		
8	x	x		
9		x		x
10	x	x		
11	x			
12	x			
13	x	x		
14		x		
15		x		
16	x			
1911–15				
1	x	x		
2			x	
3	x	x		
4	x			
5	x	x		
6	x			
7		x		
8	x			
9	x			
1916–20				
1	x	x		
2	x	x		
1931–35				
1	x			

were larger houses in the rural countryside, but they were not in the majority. The single pen house only represents a stereotype if it is interpreted in a stereotypical manner. The single pen plan house was not born solely of poverty or necessity. Rather, the big house represents a traditional way of using and understanding space. Nor may we assume that a "simple" house represents a simplicity of spatial organization. Instead we need to try to understand the complexity of little houses that are "big."

The people who once lived in single pen houses may now prefer houses in which "everything is cut to itself," but they understand and respect the pattern of life within the "big house." In describing former homes most use terms of fondness rather than the terms of anger or hostility one might expect if these were simply poor houses for poor people. Addie Norton said she cried her eyes out the day she heard her childhood home, a one-room log house, had burned. "It was not a fine house, but it was a right good house," she concluded.[87]

CHAPTER THREE

Rethinking the House:
The Double Pen Plan

The history of building and use of double pen plans in southwestern North Carolina exemplifies both the continuity of spatial systems transcending changes in form and the reorganization of spatial use within a retained traditional form. The early twentieth century was a time of profound social and cultural change in rural southwestern North Carolina. Although these changes affected the use of the single pen and center-passage plan houses, the effect of social change on domestic spatial use is perhaps most clearly understood from an examination of the double pen plan.

Examination of the use of the double pen plan also clarifies the relationship between the use of the small single pen house and the use of the much larger center-passage dwelling as parts of a single system of traditional spatial preferences within rural southwestern North Carolina. The clear relationship both types have with the double pen in terms of spatial use demonstrates that both the smallest and largest folk house types contained related systems of spatial use. Common patterns shared by the occupants of all three types of houses include the intensive utilization of a single room ("the room we lived in"), the kitchen that is either integrated into the main living space or is physically and conceptually separate, and the lack of designated bedrooms.

For the purpose of this study, "double pen" refers to any of the folk

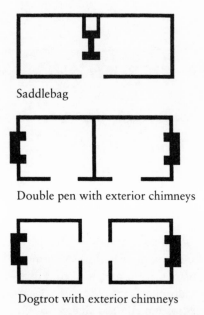

Saddlebag

Double pen with exterior chimneys

Dogtrot with exterior chimneys

Figure 20. Typical double pen plans

plans of the Upland South in which the main block of the house consists of two (more-or-less) units of equal size. In southwestern North Carolina the central chimney "saddlebag" house is far more prevalent than the double pen plan with exterior end chimneys. The "dogtrot" house is a clearly related building variant, although the presence of the open passage also makes it akin to the center-passage I-house in spatial use. While a few dogtrot houses do survive in southwestern North Carolina, most are early and all have been enclosed. No oral testimony was available on the spatial use of this plan in its original form.

Variations within the double pen plans are numerous. Surviving examples are of log, plank (boxed), or frame construction. Some were created as a result of addition, others built as a whole. Early examples of those not built as part of an additive process still tended to be composed of two separate construction units while later examples were built as

Figure 21. Enclosed log dogtrot house. Henry Stevens Carson House, mid-nineteenth century, Buncombe County, N.C. (North Carolina Division of Archives and History, Western Office; photograph by Mary Jo Brezny).

an integrated whole. Early examples invariably have two "front" doors, while later saddlebags often have a single symmetrically placed doorway. Double pen plan houses can be one, one-and-a-half, or two stories in height. A double pen plan house may have no separate kitchen, a kitchen in a completely separate structure, or an attached rear ell or shed kitchen.

In interviewing people about these houses, it initially appeared that no clear folk typology distinguishes between variants of the double pen houses, or for that matter between double pen houses and houses of other plans. Often only intensive questioning clarified the type discussed in the interview. Of course, it would not be expected that most individuals would use the terminology of folk architecture scholars, but they seemed to lack any comparable system of labeling the various house

Figure 22. Log saddlebag house built as part of additive process. E. K. Roberts House, early nineteenth century, Buncombe County, N.C. (North Carolina Division of Archives and History, Western Office; photograph by Mary Jo Brezny).

plans.[1] Local builders, however, obviously recognized and built a limited number of types. A system clearly existed and, if pressed, most people distinguished house types by certain definable features.

Individuals in southwestern North Carolina usually identify the double pen plan by two features. One is the presence of two fireplaces in the main block of the house (excluding the kitchen). The saddlebag plan is usually described as a house with a "double fireplace," "double chimney," or "stacked chimney."[2] The other feature is the presence of two rooms of equal size. R. O. Wilson of Wilson Creek in Jackson County described the type of house his grandfather built in these terms: "Built a big frame house and have a chimney in the center. Have two fireplaces in

Figure 23. Later saddlebag dwelling built as an integrated whole. Wash Hutchinson House, Henderson County, N.C. (North Carolina Division of Archives and History, Western Office; photograph by the author).

it, one room have one, you go into the other room and there'd be a room in there with a fireplace. Double chimney, double fireplace, you see. You could live in either end of the house, if you wanted to."[3] As R. O. Wilson indicates, in the double pen house only one room was actually the room you "lived" in, but it was not physically distinguished from the other main room of the house. Eller Garrett described her childhood home in these terms: "One end of it was a log house, and the other end was an old plank house. And a chimney in the middle."[4] Nanny Sorrells also said of her childhood home, built of logs by her grandfather: "It was more than two rooms, it was like two houses, all put together. But the chimney, one of the big chimneys, was in the center."[5] Finally,

Fanny Fisher recalled: "Well, my granddaddy and them, they had two chimneys to their house. And kept a fire in both houses."[6]

The description of double pen dwellings as consisting of two "houses" is apt particularly for those homes built of log or created by the process of addition, but it also reflects the various traditional meanings of the word "house." Some functional structures were referred to as "houses" (such as springhouse or smokehouse), but "house" could also refer to a specific room within the dwelling.

Most double pen houses were also described in terms emphasizing their relatively large size, as in the case of Mrs. Fisher who spoke of her grandfather's "great long house,"[7] or Jessie Frazier who described her grandparents' home as a "big double log house."[8] In many turn-of-the-century mountain communities in the region, these probably were the largest homes, as the larger central-passage plan houses tended to be confined to the relatively prosperous valley land.

Speculations on the origin of the double pen plans tend to suggest either that the plans were logical solutions to building, or adding to, a log house, or that the various subtypes were products of Old World traditions.[9] Studies of the antecedents of the double pen plans do not usually account for spatial use, assuming, perhaps, that use is inevitably linked to plan or would follow its course of diffusion. Whether the double pen plans have continental European origins or are independent inventions of the Upland South, the traditional spatial use of these houses in southwestern North Carolina clearly reflects a British heritage. True hall and parlor plans were not built in southwestern North Carolina, but oral testimony indicates that traditionally the two primary rooms in the double pen plans were used in ways equivalent to the use of the British-derived hall and parlor.

The individual who chose to build a double pen house (without a separate kitchen) was accepting a system of spatial use which was different from that of the person whose two rooms were a "big house and kitchen." Both single pen and double pen plans did share a single intensively used room similar in function to the post-medieval hall. In the double pen plan this room was referred to as "the room we lived in," "the house," or "the fireplace room." [10] The other room of the double pen plan was traditionally the parlor. Unlike the small "other room" of the partitioned single pen dwelling, the room ostensibly had a formal purpose. [11] It is difficult for individuals with modern domestic spatial values to comprehend that in a house with few rooms, one of the two main rooms would be designated for formal purposes, while there would be no room designated as a "bedroom" and possibly no separate kitchen. The additional space was formal rather than private or strictly functional.

As mentioned previously, one of the features most commonly associated with the double pen plan is the presence of two fireplaces in the main block of the house. The presence of a second hearth was critical in separating formal functions away from the main hearth. It was the presence of this hearth, and not the size of the rooms, that functionally distinguished the double pen from the partitioned single pen house. Monroe Ledford of the Union community in Macon County remembered: "Usually the back room was the parlor. Yeah, that's the way it was at our place. I guess that's the way it was all over the country. . . . That is if it was built with a fireplace or something in it." Asked what the case was if they did not have a fireplace, he responded, "Well, I don't guess they called that a parlor. It wouldn't be a very nice place to entertain company if it's cold you know." [12]

The degree to which people actually used the second fireplace varied. Fanny Fisher recalled that her granddaddy kept a fire "in both houses," but a neighbor "had two fireplaces, one on each side, you know, of the chimney. Just one chimney, but two fireplaces. . . . They never did have a fire in one room, as I've ever seen." [13] Asked if both fireplaces were used in most saddlebag houses, Vestal Cochran responded, "That depended on the amount of wood they had. Most of the time they didn't use the second one unless they had company. Because they got their wood, you know, a day at a time. They didn't have a lot ahead." [14]

In many households the parlor absorbed relatively little of the day to day activities. The parlor was "for company"; family, and often friends and neighbors, socialized around the hearth in the other room. Formal "company" most frequently consisted of the visiting preacher. Other formal uses of the parlor included courting, marriages or funerals, and sometimes dancing if permitted by the mores of the family and community. Many families maintained this formal space despite the fact that actual use was sporadic.

The seeming exception to the lack of everyday use of the parlor was the common presence of a bed or beds in the room. The use of the parlor as a sleeping room is in keeping, however, with a duality that developed in post-medieval England in which the parlor could be used either as a best sleeping chamber or a formal sitting room.[15] In seventeenth-century New England and the coastal South, the parlor served both functions.[16] The presence of the beds, however, did not necessarily detract from the formality of the parlor in southwestern North Carolina. In many instances, beds were part of the parlor's formal role, as the room was reserved not only for formal "sitting," but also for the sleeping of guests. As one man explained during the course of a story: "So [the visitor] finally decided to spend the night, and we put him in the preacher's room. That was the parlor in those days. When company come and preacher would stay, see when preacher come over there, he'd come in a buggy, and he couldn't go back that day, and he'd spend the night with us."[17] While the parlor was commonly associated with sleeping company, some families also slept family members in the parlor. Despite this fact, the formal identity of the parlor was still maintained. Monroe Ledford, for instance, noted of the parlor in his childhood home, "Oh yeah, we had beds in it. But they called it the parlor. Mostly a company room." Parlors in his community were decorated a little nicer than the living rooms, they were sometimes used for dances (with the furniture removed), and they were used to sleep company. Mr. Ledford noted, however, that the parlor was also used to sleep members of the family. "I'm just trying to think of a separate parlor with nothing in it, no bed. I just can't think of a house in the community, to tell you the truth.'Cause most people had reasonable big families. Their houses were small. They just didn't have that much room."[18] The parlor, however, was seldom the parents' bedroom. It served instead in the more peripheral role of a room to sleep children. Traditionally, the living room was the preferred location of the head of the household's bed.

These facts suggest that the formal role of the parlor was in fact more developed than its private role. The sleeping of guests was thought of as part of this formal role, and the choice to sleep children in the parlor, rather than use it as the parents' bedroom, provided less conflict to the room's formal identity. The use of the room for sleeping did not unduly detract from its formality, nor do the dual functions necessarily suggest generalized room use. The *idea* of the parlor was still formal. In essence, by permitting the room to be used for sleeping but by not defining it as a bedroom, the system maximized privacy while still retaining a large portion of the house for formal purposes.[19] Although in many families actual use of the parlor was more often private (sleeping of a family member) than formal, individuals still defined the parlor as "special for company." The idealized social use more clearly defined the room than its actual use.[20]

The living room ("room we lived in") and the parlor were the essential core of the double pen house. As with the single pen and center-passage plans, the upstairs of the double pen house, when present, tended to be viewed as peripheral and was used somewhat reluctantly.[21] When asked if her childhood home was two stories in height, Anna Collett, who had been one of eleven children, responded, "Yeah, we had to have beds upstairs."[22] If necessary, the upstairs was used to sleep children, but generally not adults or guests.

The separate kitchen was a common, but not essential, part of the double pen plan. During the nineteenth century, the separate kitchen was frequently completely detached, connected by an open breezeway, or was adjacent to the house, but was not provided with an interior doorway.[23] By the early twentieth century, the majority of double pen houses probably had a kitchen. While the growing preference for a kitchen may be interpreted as the separation of cooking and eating from the domestic center of the house (also isolating the duties of the woman from the dwelling's social core), the kitchen itself was less likely to be detached from the house.[24] By the early twentieth century, the kitchen was being treated less as an outbuilding and more (physically and conceptually) as an integrated part of the dwelling. This dual trend toward having the kitchen as a separate room but still an integrated part of the house took place in the early twentieth century in all of the common folk plans in southwestern North Carolina.

Following soon after the trend toward a separate but integrated kitchen were other changes that would radically alter the hall and parlor spatial arrangement of the double pen plan. Still, it is evident that this traditional arrangement of space persisted well into living memory. The double pen plan is different from the classic hall and parlor plan in that the sizes of the rooms do not suggest their function; as R. O. Wilson said, "You could live in either end." The enlarging of the parlor to equal the size of the living room does not appear to be related to changes in spatial use; if anything, the parlor was spatially under-utilized. Nor would the demands of log building necessarily result in the symmetry of the double pen plan. Rather, there seems to be, from the earliest known Anglo-American building in southwestern North Carolina, simply a preference for the basic symmetry of two equal-sized "houses" rather than the asymmetry of the Old World house types.[25] The accompanying system of spatial use, however, proved to be far more conservative, transcending the changes in form, and perhaps persisting in the use of the double pen plan in this region longer than it did in the mainstream tidewater South where true hall and parlor plans were built.[26]

Understanding the use of the double pen plan also gives us a better appreciation for the nature of building and social life in rural southwestern North Carolina. Folk building in this region was not an architecture of poverty characterized chiefly by over-crowding and lack of privacy. The builder who chose the double pen plan, or expanded a single pen house into a double pen house, was not trying to alleviate a lack of "living" space but was creating a large formal space. These were not the antisocial mountaineers of popular stereotypes, but were individuals for whom socializing was an important element of their lives and the parlor an important symbol. The majority of individuals interviewed described a rather intense pattern of visiting during their childhoods.

While socializing could take place in the "big house," those who could afford a larger house built an arena for formal activity (even if many types of socializing continued to take place in the living room). Visiting within many mountain communities, where travel was difficult even in the early twentieth century, often demanded that visitors sleep overnight. As part of the formal role of the parlor, provisions were made to sleep visitors, but the system was flexible enough so that to increase privacy family members might also use the beds in the parlor without threatening the formal nature of the room. Therefore, while the use of the double pen plan house demonstrates an intensely conservative pattern of spatial organization, spatial use also made sense in terms of the regional patterns of social interaction.

In describing the culturally conservative patterns of domestic spatial use and folk building in southwestern North Carolina, however, caution must be taken not to overemphasize the uniqueness or "otherness" of this region or southern Appalachia in general. The majority of data on the spatial use of traditional houses comes from mainstream New England and the white population of the tidewater South where the forces of cultural change were felt very early. There is relatively little data from other cultural groups. George McDaniel's study of rural African-Americans in southeastern Maryland, however, suggests that during the nineteenth and early twentieth centuries these Marylanders shared many patterns of spatial use with the white Appalachians of southwestern North Carolina.[27] Far more extensive studies are needed before conclusions can be reached on the distribution of these spatial patterns. In the study of other folk traditions, such as ballad singing, popular and scholarly attention to the culturally conservative nature of southern Appalachia has sometimes obscured recognition of similar traditions in other parts of the country. Comparative data from other parts of rural America may well prove that Appalachia is not as uniquely conservative as it is often portrayed.

So far, the ability of a conservative pattern of spatial use to withstand change in architectural form has been described. Even as a new Anglo-American building system developed in southern Appalachia, individuals clung to a conservative, British-derived system of domestic spatial use. By the turn of the century, however, the opposite began to happen. Patterns of spatial use began to change within the double pen house while the folk plan remained relatively unchanged, at least for a few decades.

As already described, the separation of cooking and eating from the other functions of "the room we lived in" was one aspect of spatial change within the double pen house. (However, a small portion of the population had already accepted this change by the early twentieth century, as the separate kitchen was an option throughout most of the nineteenth century.) Obviously, this was a change that came gradually in the region and did not radically challenge the basic spatial arrangement of the double pen plan house.

The traditional parlor, rather than the living room, was most vulnerable to the forces of cultural change. Responses about the nature of the parlor during the interviews indicated that spatial change affected different families and communities at different times. As with the use of the term "big house," the designation of one of the rooms within the double pen plan as a "parlor" is not necessarily predictable according to the informant's absolute age or the location of the individual's community. For instance, one would suspect that the oldest informants and those who grew up in the most remote communities would be most likely to describe conservative "hall and parlor" patterns of spatial use. This was not always the case. Monroe Ledford, born in 1909, provided a detailed account of use of the traditional parlor in Union, a relatively accessible community south of Franklin, the Macon County seat.[28] On the other hand, Anna Collett, born ten years earlier and raised in Aquone, a far more remote community in the same county, associated the term "parlor" with the homes of rich folks and not with the double pen house she was raised in.[29] Obviously, the factors that affect change within a family or community's system of domestic spatial use are complex. The traditional presence of a parlor may have persisted longer in communities where there were a large number of double pen plan houses rather than in those where single pen plans dominated. This would be one reason for a more traditional pattern of use within a comparatively less remote community.

The evidence does suggest that during the early twentieth century there was a rapid decline in the use of the term "parlor" in reference to the rural double pen house. This change took place during the lifetime of most of the individuals interviewed. Increasingly, the term "parlor" took on its more modern meaning as an exclusively formal room found in larger houses. Aspects of traditional use of the parlor, however, may have persisted even after the term became associated only with larger non-folk houses. Vestal Cochran, for instance, called the room a bed-room, although she noted that a fire would be built in its fireplace if the family had company.[30] Essie Moore remembers that her grandmother had a "guest room" in her home, a two-story double pen plan house with end chimneys and without a separate kitchen. The room had two beds and a fireplace that held a fire only when company came. "Nobody ever got in there, only when somebody comes. She had it fixed up real good." After the death of her grandmother, Essie Moore's family moved from their one-room house into the larger house and the "guest room" became her grandfather's room.[31] While there may have been some con-tinued use of the parlor for formal purposes after the term itself became primarily used for non-folk dwellings, the trend during the twentieth century was toward stripping the room of its formal functions. The room increasingly became the "other room" or "back room" and was used for sleeping.

Tracing changes in the use of "the room we lived in" is even more difficult due to the original vagueness of room nomenclature. Several individuals, lacking a definite name for this room, labeled the room a "bedroom" or "kitchen" although they might also describe the room as the family's "living quarters." Essie Moore, for instance, referred to the other large room in her grandmother's house first as a kitchen, then later as the "living quarters."[32] It is difficult in many instances to tell when the original room names are being used or if modern terms are being ap-plied retrospectively. The modern term "living room" is sometimes used for this room; the meaning, however, was more literal in reference to traditional use. The problem of establishing room nomenclature is evident in a conversation with Lolita Dean about the turn-of-the-century saddlebag house she was raised in and still lives in. Asked what a room was called, she responded, "Oh, I don't know, we just called it a room." (Interviewer: "Just a room?") "Yes, just. We used it as setting room or we used it as a bedroom. We had to use it as a bedroom, and we kept it, you know, just as it is." [33] (The room is still furnished with both an organ and a bed.) While people clearly know the functions of the various rooms in their house, they often were unconcerned with specific room names that denoted function.

Changes in room nomenclature do suggest some changes in spatial use. As the use of the term "parlor" declined in reference to the double pen plan, there was a rise in use of the terms "sitting room" (or "setting room") and "front room" in reference to the living room. The adoption of these more formal terms, which are sometimes also used in reference to a parlor, reflects the living room's absorption of the formal functions of the parlor. Initially, however, the role of the living room changed less than that of the parlor. Even after the other room ceased to be a parlor, the living room generally continued as both the parents' bedroom and the family gathering room. The pattern of use described by Anna Collett in her childhood home, a frame saddlebag house, follows this general pattern, except that her family routinely utilized the second fireplace: "And us young'uns in the wintertime, we'd all gather around in this bedroom, fireplace, and pop corn, and have a big time." [34] Other families seldom used the second fireplace in their double pen houses if the room served solely as a bedroom.

In the alteration of the "hall and parlor" spatial arrangement of the double pen plan house, a less common option seems to have been exercised by a few individuals who lived closer to town and were more affected by mainstream spatial patterns. Rather than eliminate the parlor, these people followed the pattern found in turn-of-the-century American towns by making the parlor even more formal and specialized. This was far more common among those who lived in rural center-passage houses, but evidence suggests that it sometimes took place in the double pen plan house as well. Leo Gibson of Cowee, for instance, noted that the parlor in her childhood home was originally used to sleep company. The living room or front room was "where we set of a night." After the children got old enough to court, however, the beds were removed from the parlor and the room became "just a courting room." [35] As no one else mentioned the inappropriateness of beds within a traditional parlor used for courting, this suggests the adoption of Victorian standards associated with mainstream turn-of-the-century parlors. Also from the Cowee community, Eula Bryson reported that in 1910 her family added a parlor to their rural house, "for the girls got big enough to court." The new parlor also contained an organ. The living room, however, continued to be used in a conservative manner: "We still had a bed in that too. It was quite a big room, and there was a bed in that where my father and mother slept." [36]

As the front room or living room began to absorb the formal functions of the parlor, many families no longer felt that it was the appropriate place for the parents' bed. Some eliminated beds altogether from this room, although this move was not universal, and one occasionally still sees beds in living rooms in western North Carolina.

Monroe Ledford's comparison of his childhood home with the house he moved to after he married exemplifies the changes that took place in the use of the double pen plan dwelling during the early twentieth century. The houses were similar in plan: "Two rooms downstairs, a stacked chimney in the middle. Kitchen and dining room lean-to on this side. Two bedrooms upstairs." The rooms in his father's house had consisted of "a front room, the parlor, the kitchen and dining room, and the upstairs." Asked if he also had a parlor in the house he lived in after he married, he responded, "No, the front room, we called it there. We had beds in the back room and upstairs." While Mr. Ledford equated the old parlor with the new front room that had absorbed some of its formal functions, the front room was also the family gathering room and was not specifically designated, in daytime use, "only for company." And despite the presence of a second hearth, the "back room" of Monroe Ledford's later house was simply used as a sleeping room.[37]

The use of the functionally vague terms "front room" and "back room" that marked the transition from the hall and parlor spatial arrangement to the living room–bedroom organization also equated the use of the double pen house with that of the partitioned single pen plan, breaking down the social distinctions that once had been inherent in the difference between their spatial pattern of use. Practically, the front room–back room system seemed to make little sense in reference to the double pen plan, for both rooms were the same size and were equally accessible physically from the front door or doors. Nor could "front" and "back" be oriented to a single hearth as it is in the single pen plan house. In terms of the changing social use of the double pen plan, however, front room and back room do make sense as the hearth in the front room became the social center of the house and the front room was socially, if not physically, more accessible than the back room.

The changes in spatial use of the double pen plan came incrementally with many aspects of change pre-dating the decline in building the form itself. Some individuals continued to build double pen plan houses, although they no longer used the hall and parlor spatial arrangement. Just as important, however, is the fact that people continued to live in old houses. Too often in examining architecture as an artifact of social change, conclusions are drawn from building norms rather than housing norms. Changes in building, even if they are socially induced, do not lead to the total abandonment of old structures. Only a segment of the total population is usually living in new houses; the others muddle along with their anachronistic dwellings. Social changes sometimes bring the physical alteration of houses to suit new needs.[38] The example of the double pen plan, however, clearly demonstrates that people can continue to live in unaltered houses without being tied to old forms of spatial use. Profound spatial changes occurred without the physical alteration of the double pen plan house. Spatial change was characterized not by rebuilding or remodeling but by the "rethinking" of the house.[39]

The alteration of a spatial system without physical alteration of the house again exemplifies the independence of spatial use and form. Although during the early twentieth century both traditional architectural use and form were affected by social change, the nature of the impact was quite separate. Traditional form could, and did, accommodate changing spatial patterns, and the decline of traditional building did not prevent the continued use of traditional dwellings.

By the 1920s and 1930s "popular" style houses were rapidly replacing folk dwellings in southwestern North Carolina. After a generation of technological change, as well as change in social patterns of building, folk form finally met its demise. The new acceptance of architectural forms inspired by popular style suggests a relinquishing of control over architectural forms that could be suited to regional patterns of spatial use. Perhaps this was appropriate, for the rural inhabitants of southwestern North Carolina were also relinquishing a traditional system of spatial use in preference for mainstream twentieth-century patterns. The house form most widely accepted as the replacement for the small rural folk house, however, does reflect some continuity of traditional spatial preferences.

The small "southern bungalow" with its front facing gable looks radically different from the traditional houses of the region, although it found widespread acceptance in rural southwestern North Carolina during the third and fourth decades of the twentieth century. It is not a product of local folk design.[40] The interior arrangement of the house, two rooms side by side with a kitchen to the rear, however, must have been comfortably familiar to those individuals who adopted the new house type. The most important spatial change was not in the relative proportions of the rooms, but in the lack of the open hearth in many of these houses. The willingness of rural individuals to finally relinquish the open hearth and the social meanings attached to it facilitated the acceptance of the bungalow plan. (One does, on occasion, see front-

Figure 24. Front-gable southern bungalow. Hiram Tallent House, ca. 1939, Macon County, N.C. (Photograph by the author).

gable bungalows with a stone chimney attached to a non-gable side.) The spatial use of these bungalows was, in fact, quite similar to that which evolved in the "rethinking" of the double pen plan house. During the 1930s individuals living in "modern" bungalows were practicing patterns of domestic room use similar to those of their neighbors who continued to live in older saddlebag and partitioned single pen houses (particularly as stoves were replacing open hearths even in these older houses).

Despite what appear to be major breaks in building traditions during the early to mid-twentieth century in southwestern North Carolina, individuals who lived through this period of change often focus on the continuities. The changes seem to them to be slow and incremental in nature. Rural bungalows are seldom distinguished as being signifi-

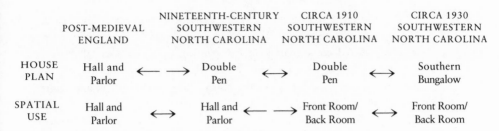

Figure 25. Continuities and discontinuities in house plan and spatial use

cantly different from "folk" houses, even by older individuals, and many now accept bungalows as being "old-time" houses.[41] Several individuals noted continuities in use between their childhood folk houses and their later non-folk dwellings (the distinction is mine, based on their description, and was not made by the individuals interviewed). Anna Collett, for instance, saw several continuities in use of the double pen house she was raised in and her later, circa 1925, non-folk house. One similarity was in the presence of beds in the living room. Speaking of her childhood home, she said, "We had one bed in the living room, no we had two beds in the living room. Yeah, we had two. When I was raising my family here, we had a bed here in the living room. I had nine [children]."[42]

In the early twentieth century plank replaced log as the preferred construction technique among many rural people. For those forced to work off the farm, this fast construction technique facilitated the continuation of cooperative building among members of a community or family. Even after the change of form, some of the early bungalows continued to be cooperatively or self built. This balancing of change and continuity in spatial use, architectural form, technology, and social building patterns made major changes in local building appear incremental and therefore palatable to the local builders and users of architecture.

Overall the history of the double pen house in southwestern North Carolina shows a balance of continuities and discontinuities in house plan and spatial use. Periods of discontinuity in house plan are marked by continuity in spatial use, while the major change in spatial use was countered by a period of stability in house plan. The trend is neither wholly toward conservatism or innovation but a balance of the two. By understanding this balance, rather than focusing only on physical changes, we may better comprehend the nature of tradition and change in folk architecture.

CHAPTER FOUR

The Center Passage: Conflict in Function

During the nineteenth century the majority of folk houses in southwestern North Carolina were small. Larger traditional houses were not common except in the fertile river valleys. Impressive two-story double pen houses were sometimes built, but the plan of choice for most traditional builders who desired a larger house had a pair of exterior end chimneys, central passages on both the first and second floors, and was a single room in depth. These dwellings, sometimes referred to by scholars as "I-houses," are similar to traditional houses found throughout many parts of the rural United States.[1]

The center-passage I-house in southwestern North Carolina must have presented quite a contrast to small single pen dwellings. Unlike the latter, the I-houses were commonly frame and were usually painted. Although they might only have four rooms, their facade was impressive, and they tended to look much bigger than they actually were. Spatial use would also seem to be significantly different. Center passages, it has been hypothesized, represent a formalization of social relationships. The center door leads to the hallway, rather than to the main living area, suggesting a socially "closed" rather than "open" plan. The visitor was denied immediate access to the hearth and was instead left in a formal unlived-in space that operated as a "social lock."[2]

Certainly the builders of center-passage I-houses communicated

something different about their social and economic status than those
dwellers of humbler log houses. However, oral testimony suggests that
at least by the late nineteenth and early twentieth centuries, spatial use
was not as radically different as it initially appears. Continuities are
found in the spatial use of all the common folk houses of southwestern
North Carolina. For the inhabitants of the center-passage house, however, these continuities seem to have come at a price. The center-passage
house in this region presents an intriguing example of the acceptance of
a house plan that is not fully compatible with the patterns of spatial use
of its inhabitants.

    The appearance of center-passage plans in the
repertoire of American folk builders has been attributed to a variety of
reasons ranging from the ability of the center hallway to cool a house to
radical cultural, social, and mental changes of the eighteenth century.[3]
In southwestern North Carolina, environmental concerns would have
been less critical as summers are relatively cool. Nor can the appearance
of the I-house in this region be seen to coincide with a rationalization
of the eighteenth-century mind. The pioneer conditions of the late eighteenth and early nineteenth centuries in southwestern North Carolina
generally precluded the building of large frame houses. Until the mid-
nineteenth century building options, even for the elite, were limited.
Undoubtedly, there were social distinctions even in the pioneer conditions of early nineteenth-century southwestern North Carolina, but
in practice, individuals had limited means of expressing them architecturally and perhaps could ill-afford to create barriers between themselves and their neighbors. Those who desired and could afford a more
distinguished house simply built large double pen log homes. One of
the rare surviving examples from this period is the large log saddlebag
house built by John Orr near Etowah (present day Henderson County)
around 1820.
    A decade after Orr built his home the economic and social situation
began to change. The opening of the Buncombe Turnpike in 1828 connected southwestern North Carolina to markets in Tennessee and South

Figure 26. John Orr House, massive log saddlebag, ca. 1820, Henderson County, N.C. (North Carolina Division of Archives and History, Western Office; photograph by Michael Southern).

Carolina. The building of the turnpike and the improvement of roads within the region made farming the river valleys commercially profitable and attracted new settlers, many of them slaveholders, to southwestern North Carolina. By the 1840s, and particularly the 1850s, slave ownership had taken a dramatic upswing in the region.[4] Coincidental with the rapid rise in slave ownership and the increased market orientation of agriculture during these two decades was the introduction of the center-passage I-house as the symbol of a developing rural elite.

The builders of center-passage I-houses came from several groups. Some were original pioneers who had prospered in business, politics, or agriculture. While many of these builders simply expanded their single pen log houses into center-passage I-houses, others built new frame dwellings in the classic, two-story, five-bay, center-passage plan. (A few local builders rejected the I-house form but built new one-story frame structures with center passages.) The sons of those who had invested early in the rich river valley land also prospered after the opening of the turnpike. Robert Orr built, with slave labor, a large frame I-house downriver from his parents' log house.

The growing prosperity of pre–Civil War western North Carolina not only led to rebuilding among some early pioneers and their families but also brought a new wave of settlement to the region. New settlers to river valley land in western North Carolina were often from well-to-do families in the piedmont or lowland South. The Mills River valley in Henderson County attracted several South Carolina families. Unlike the very wealthy lowlanders who had already established a summer colony in the county at Flat Rock, these settlers became a more integral part of the rural society as they became involved in local political and economic affairs. The newly opened Cherokee lands further west also attracted those who could afford large tracts of river valley land. The three prominent slave owning families along the Hiwassee River in Cherokee County, the Harshaws, Sudderths, and McCombs, were all well-to-do emigrants from Burke County in North Carolina's western piedmont.[5] Unlike the early pioneers, the river valley landowners who settled in the 1840s and 1850s built frame I-houses as their first dwellings.

Neither the plantations nor the plantation houses of this new rural class in western North Carolina were particularly impressive by lowland standards. The planter might have owned between twenty and forty slaves, possibly using some of them in business enterprises other than agriculture.[6] These planters' homes would have seemed modest in many parts of the South. Still, the two-story, five-bay, center-passage houses that became a symbol of this class must have been impressive compared to local building norms. The individuals who built these houses were not fabulously wealthy, but they did form a relatively narrow elite in southwestern North Carolina's rural society.

The upswing in economic and social diversification of the 1840s and

Figure 27. Robert Orr House, center-passage I-house (siding and porch altered), ca. 1850, Henderson County, N.C. (North Carolina Division of Archives and History, Western Office; photograph by the author).

Figure 28. Mills River antebellum I-house (fenestration and porch altered). Ladson House, ca. 1850, Henderson County, N.C. (North Carolina Division of Archives and History, Western Office; photograph by the author).

1850s was terminated by war in the 1860s. Southwestern North Carolina was spared the large battles, but the war was truly civil. Throughout western North Carolina loyalties were split, generally along social and geographical lines, with the slave owners living in I-houses along the river valleys supporting the Confederacy and the people in the mountainous areas where small log houses were the norm often supporting the Union. In counties such as Cherokee one still can collect from the descendants of these two distinct groups family stories of the horrors perpetrated by either "yankees" or "rebels."[7]

After the war the promise of rural prosperity failed as western North Carolina shared in the economic depression of the rest of the South. The Western North Carolina Railroad, chartered in the 1850s, was delayed for decades by the political confusion and corruption of the postwar era. The fate of the old planter class was divided. Some became successful businessmen oriented to town life rather than agriculture; others were absorbed socially into the mainstream rural society. In Cherokee County, for example, Abram McDowell Harshaw, son of Abram Harshaw, the largest slaveholder in the County, became a prominent banker after the war and in 1880 built a large non-traditional house on the family property along the Hiwassee River. Many of the next generation of Sudderths, however, remained farmers and built modest vernacular dwellings on land that was formerly the Sudderth plantation.[8]

The center-passage house did not disappear with the dissolution of the planter elite. Rather, it found a growing acceptance among the rural middle class. Post–Civil War center-passage houses were more modest than their antebellum predecessors. They usually have a three-bay instead of a five-bay facade and are occasionally only a story and a half or a single story in height. The smaller center-passage house did not, however, replace the single and double pen system of building even among the rural middle class. In fact, both systems of building coexisted and flourished through the late nineteenth and early twentieth centuries.

The coexistence of the "closed" center-passage plan with the socially "open" single and double pen houses raises questions about the actual meaning and use of the center hallway in southwestern North Carolina rural society. Unlike the planter elite who built the majority of the antebellum I-houses, the builders of the later center-passage houses did not constitute a separate class of society. They may have been generally better off than the inhabitants of the smaller single pen houses, but there is relatively little to distinguish them from their neighbors who built double pen houses. From oral testimony we know of families who moved from single pen or double pen houses to center-passage houses or from houses with center hallways to smaller dwellings. The parents or siblings of builders of center-passage houses sometimes lived in smaller folk dwellings.[9] Within this social situation, one wonders if it is conceivable that two separate systems of social use of space were being enforced. Were the inhabitants of center-passage houses enforcing social barriers while their neighbors and family members were not?

In southwestern North Carolina a fair number of existing center-passage plan houses have had the hallway removed. One wall of the hall is taken out so that there are two rooms of unequal size. Just as the eighteenth-century farmer in eastern Virginia and North Carolina might have converted a hall and parlor plan into a center-passage house, western North Carolinians created hall and parlor-like houses from center-passage plans.[10] In some center-passage houses built during the late nineteenth and early twentieth centuries, the alteration was made within a generation of the house's construction. When asked why her father removed the hallway from the house built by her grandfather in the 1880s, one woman responded that her family thought the space "wasted."[11]

The removal of some center hallways occurred late enough to be part of a modernization of spatial use. Modern American domestic spatial use has not favored these large formal spaces, and the removal of hallways from older houses has been noted elsewhere in the United States.[12] Some of the known removals, however, occurred during a period when center hallways were still included in some folk and many popular style houses built in western North Carolina. While "modernizing" cannot be

Figure 29. George Hayes House, center-passage dwelling with three doors on (original) front facade, mid-nineteenth century, Cherokee County, N.C. (North Carolina Division of Archives and History, Western Office; photograph by Roger Manley).

excluded as a cause of center-passage removals, there is artifactual and oral evidence suggesting that, in some instances, removal of the hallway was the result of an incompatibility of spatial use and house plan.

Variations of the ideal center-passage I-house plan suggest that, in some cases, the original builder, and not just subsequent users, might not have been comfortable with its social and spatial implications. One of the earliest variants is the building of the I-house with more than one door on the front facade. The two surviving mid-nineteenth-century I-houses in the Cowee Valley along the Little Tennessee River were built with three front doors. Another of a slightly later date is known to have existed a few miles away in the Burningtown section.[13] French Haynes remembers her grandfather's center-passage house near the Pigeon River in Haywood County as having two front doors.[14] Examples of center-

passage houses with more than one door on the front facade are also found in Cherokee and Buncombe counties.[15]

Center-passage houses that are created by additions to a single pen house are likely to have more than one front door. The house described by French Haynes was possibly originally a single pen house as the stairs were located in the living room and the house is believed to have been substantially enlarged. Enclosed dogtrot houses also sometimes have three doors on the front facade.[16] The Hall House and the Bryson House on the Little Tennessee, however, were frame houses that had not been enlarged in length. The builders of these houses seem to have followed the pattern of the older double pen plans by providing a front door to each room.

In two known cases the builders of the early multiple-door center-passage houses were early pioneers who established themselves prior to the introduction of the I-house to the region. Colonel Hall, who built his center-passage house in 1850, was a slaveholder who owned five hundred acres, but he was also an early pioneer in Macon County. The multiple-door George Hayes House in Tomotla, Cherokee County, was also built by one of that county's earliest white settlers. On the other hand, this pattern of extra doors is not found in Mills River, where the well-to-do South Carolinians who were later settlers built homes. It is probable that the early pioneers who subsequently built center-passage dwellings were more sensitive to local domestic spatial patterns than the wealthy immigrants to the region.

The multiple-door center-passage houses were probably not only a result of addition or alterations of other folk plans, or the syncretism of double pen and center-passage I-house forms, but also of a genuine desire on the part of the builder to permit social access to the house. For whatever reason the builder chose the center-passage plan, it was probably not to have the hallway operate as a formal "social lock." Obviously, oral history cannot provide the original intended use of these multiple doors and the spaces behind them; however, we do have available several oral testimonies from individuals now in their seventies and eighties about use of the plan by their grandparents.

Lolita Dean remembers that in her grandparents' house, "They had three doors in front. And each door led into a room, you could enter any room you wanted." Behind one door was the parlor or front room: "That's where she received visitors, in the front room. If she had company, they'd [have] a fire in the fireplace in there and we'd all stay in there." Use of the parlor was not overly restrictive: "The children didn't get to go in [some people's parlors] but, grandma never was like that, she let us feel free to use everything she had." Behind the center door was the hallway, and behind the third door was "grandmother's room," where the family gathered around the fire at night and where her grandmother and her grandmother's invalid son slept.[17]

A few miles away Katherine Porter was raised by her grandmother and great-aunt in her great-great-grandfather Hall's house. In this house one of the end rooms was also the parlor, although "it wasn't ever used unless somebody died and they laid the body out in there, or the preacher come, or somebody married or something." The outside door to the parlor was never open. Large double doors led from the front porch into the center hallway, and the third door led into the living room, which also contained a bed near the fireplace. The outside door to the living room was "open most of the time. They believed in keeping the doors open."[18]

In both Lolita Dean's and Katherine Porter's descriptions, the central area was conceived of as a hallway and not as a specific room. However, the center passage did not seem to be used as a formal receiving space, as one could enter the main room of the house directly, bypassing the central passage. Both women did note the cooling effect of the hallway; Lolita Dean referred to it as a "cool breezeway." From their memories of the early twentieth century, both women also associated the same item with the hallway, the sewing machine. "Now right over on this wall, well right next to that door was Aunt Kate's sewing machine. Because she could open the double doors in the hot weather and that door, and there would go through here, would be a good breeze," remembers Mrs. Porter.[19]

French Haynes, who was born in 1896, remembers a somewhat dif-

ferent spatial arrangement in her grandfather's mid-nineteenth-century I-house: "There were three rooms on the front and two of them were fairly big. The parlor wasn't large." The two large rooms were heated by exterior end chimneys, while the center "parlor," which Miss Haynes remembers to be about twelve feet across, was heated only by the adjacent rooms. Asked if the parlor was like a hallway, she responded, "Yes, a big hallway. And it was just used when company, you know a parlor. They had a parlor in those days. And it wasn't like the living room where people lived all the time. Everybody lived in this big room and the stairs went up from it." In this spatial arrangement, the center hallway that acted as a parlor is a formal space, but it is a *used* space, not a passageway that denied visitors immediate access to the domestic core of the home. Although the parlor was accessible by a door to the outside, the "front door" of the house through which most visitors entered was the outside door that led directly into the living room. (The other large room, a bedroom, did not have an exterior door.)[20]

The center-passage plan makes sense if the hall was used merely as a passageway. As a lived-in space, the hallway was narrow, and although environmentally practical in the summer, it was cold in the winter. "Great deal of wasted space in them, very hard to heat, those houses were," was French Haynes's assessment of the plan. Artifactual and oral evidence suggests that many builders of center-passage houses in southwestern North Carolina not only did not care to put social barriers between themselves and their neighbors but also were impatient with the concept of formal, non-used ("wasted") space. While some eventually removed the hallway, others struggled to make the center passage livable.

Two of the oldest frame houses in Buncombe County have center passages which have been enlarged so that the hallway is almost the same size as the flanking two rooms.[21] The use of the unheated central room in the circa 1835 Wagner House and the circa 1840 Thrash House is unknown; however, the proportions suggest something other than a passageway. The enlarged center hallway is also known in later frame houses, such as the circa 1870 Abram Evans House in Cherokee County.

Figure 30. Abram Evans House, wide center passage, ca. 1870, Cherokee County, N.C. (North Carolina Division of Archives and History, Western Office; photograph by the author).

Evans's granddaughter remembers beds being placed in the "hall" during the early twentieth century.[22] In the Evans House and several other examples, the stairs are not located in the passage, but are at the back of the house (either in a shed addition or on an outside porch). The enlarging of the passage and removal of the staircase suggest efforts to make the hallway livable by increasing the living space. The presence of beds in the hallway of the Evans House certainly suggests that at least by the early twentieth century the space was not used as a formal passageway. (It should be noted, however, that beds were found in parlors and living rooms in rural southwestern North Carolina through the early twentieth century and therefore were not the antithesis of formality that the contemporary mind might envision.)

If some builders managed to enlarge the center passage to a livable size, the hallway still had no direct source of heat. The exterior end chimneys of the center-passage house, even if both were kept going, must have provided a meager amount of heat to the center hallway during the winter. At least one builder tried to solve this problem. Around 1906 Samuel Stewart of Andrews, North Carolina, built a two-story center-passage house, after tearing down his grandfather's circa 1847 single-story center-passage house (which is said to have been one of the first frame houses in Cherokee County).[23] Stewart built his house with a single interior chimney that served two fireplaces, one in the northern room and one in the center passage. The other room flanking the passage was heated by a stove. Although the hallway was subsequently removed, and the fireplace is now non-functional, the original hallway mantle is still in place. Samuel Stewart also built his house so that the stairs were at the back of the house. Polly McGuire, Stewart's daughter who still lives in the house, confirms that the hallway was intended as a room. Prior to the removal of the hallway it served as the family's "sitting room" and was furnished with straight-back chairs.[24] Similar center-passage plan houses with single off-center chimneys are found elsewhere in western North Carolina, particularly in Haywood County.[25]

As we have seen, artifactual evidence, supported by oral testimony, suggests that builders of center-passage houses did not always use the hallway as a formal passage or as a social lock. Builders such as Colonel Hall, George Hayes, Humphrey Posey Haynes, James Bryson, and Julius McCoy all had homes built that allowed immediate access into the living room, the center of family activity and often a sleeping room for family members. Abram Evans and Samuel Stewart both altered the plan of the center-passage house to make the hallway livable. This alteration suggests that the attitude that a formal center passageway is "wasted space" is not purely a modern one. Despite the social significance attributed to the center passage, oral testimony of spatial use of center-passage houses during the late nineteenth and early twentieth centuries also suggests that this system of use was not substantially different from the use of smaller "socially open" folk plans. Although the actual use of the hallway varies in these descriptions, the attitudes about appropriate use of space in the center hallway house are very similar to those described by individuals who grew up in other folk houses.

Bass Hyatt, who was born in 1889, is one of the few individuals left who can provide direct testimony about life in a center-passage house at the end of the nineteenth century. Except for a few years when he lived in a smaller house after his mother remarried, he was raised in the single-story frame center-passage house built by his grandfather, Hugh Harvey Davidson, after the Civil War. As in the smaller folk houses, the center-passage Davidson House had a "room where we lived." The center passage of the Davidson House, as described by Bass Hyatt, was conceived of as a "hall." The furniture that Mr. Hyatt remembers in the hallway, however, does not suggest formality. A washstand with a bowl and pitcher, a mirror, and a dresser were the items found in this space. The room at the other end of the house was the parlor: "Special for company, you know. When they had company, go in there, and set. Then, if there were any girls around, if there were any girls, that was the courting room. Take their fiddles in there, you know, and sit and court. Didn't use to have automobiles and they had to have a parlor, you know, to court in." The parlor in the Davidson House also had beds to sleep visitors. "Company beds was back there, in the parlor. That was for when people come."[26]

The similarities with traditional spatial patterns within the double pen plan house are obvious. Different designations are used, but as in smaller folk houses, family life in a center-passage house also centered around the hearth in a single room. (Most individuals interviewed testified that the other fireplace was used only on special occasions.) The main room was where everybody gathered at night. Often it also contained a bed or beds, usually belonging to the parents or the eldest members of the household. In Lolita Dean's description of her grandparents' house, her grandmother's room was also the living room. French Haynes also said that her mother's bedroom "was really our family living room."[27] Most central-passage houses had rear kitchens; sometimes, as in Lolita Dean's and Katherine Porter's descriptions, the kitchen was a separate log structure. In the absence of a kitchen, however, cooking and eating also took place in the main room. Frances Bryson described the use of the center-passage James Bryson House after she married her husband: "Yes, we lived in this room. We lived in this room before we had this [rear ell] for a kitchen and dining room, we had this for a kitchen. We just lived in here, it was a living room and all." [28]

By the early twentieth century the nature of the parlor in the center-passage dwelling in southwestern North Carolina was changing. In Bass Hyatt's testimony we find a use of the parlor in a central-passage house that was very close to the traditional use of the double pen plan, while the descriptions of Katherine Porter and Lolita Dean indicated more formal parlors that did not accommodate sleeping as part of their functions. One might hypothesize that the use of the center passage as a parlor or formal sitting room, as described by Polly Stewart McGuire or French Haynes, might reflect an effort not only to utilize "wasted space," but also to affect a split between formal space (the parlor) and private space (the bedroom). By moving the parlor to the hallway a larger private space could be defined in the house.

In a testimony of use during a slightly later era, we find a center-passage house that, similar to some early twentieth-century double pen plan houses, does not have a separate space defined for formal use. In 1921 Oma Jenkins and her husband moved into a center-passage house in Stecoah. The plan was not too common in mountainous Graham County. "You could see them once in a while. You didn't see many with a hall then." The house had been expanded from a single pen log house and was covered with weatherboarding. "This living room now was just a log, big old log house." Oma Jenkins's daughter described the house as having three front doors, a big porch across the front, and a central entry hall. Off the hall on one side was a big living room with a fireplace and on the left side of the hall was a large bedroom that would hold about three beds. Upstairs were two more large bedrooms and off the living room there was a dining room, a separate kitchen, and a back porch.

The entry hall, which was remembered to be ten to twelve feet across, was hardly a formal passageway. Oma Jenkins added to her daughter's description: "The stairs went up in the hallway. It was a broad hall between the living room and that bedroom, you know, downstairs. And, really, I had a three quarter bed in that hall." The hallway also contained a large trunk and a sewing machine; a sheet was hung across the back, so that the end of the hall served as a closet. Beds were also found in the rooms that flanked the hall: "We always had a bed in the living room you know, 'cause there was so much room, you know, we didn't have anything to put in it. But, most of the time I had two beds in that big back bedroom downstairs and mine didn't hardly have to sleep upstairs much."[29]

Oma Jenkins's testimony indicated another link with the usage of much smaller folk houses: the reluctance to fully utilize the upstairs. Similar to many inhabitants of smaller houses, individuals who lived in center-passage houses seemed to perceive the upstairs as being solely the domain of children. It was still considered appropriate for adults to sleep in the large rooms on the first floor. Oma Jenkins had beds in every downstairs room (including the hallway) except the separate kitchen and dining room so that no one had to sleep upstairs unless they wanted to. The reluctance to fully utilize the upstairs suggests that the building of small houses and the layering of functions in a single room was indeed a result of cultural preference rather than economic limitations.[30]

While use of the hallway varied, none of the individuals who had experienced traditional center-passage houses described a system of usage where the hallway acted as a formal, unlived-in, passageway. The individuals who did describe hallways used in this manner were instead occupants of large popular style houses built during the early twentieth century. These non-traditional center-passage frame houses were generally asymmetrical, rambling, and had hipped roofs. With ten to twelve rooms in them, they would seem to represent a radical change in spatial preference from the traditional norms. For most rural western North Carolinians who built them, however, these large houses were a financial investment. "I reckon they built this house big enough 'til they could

Figure 31. Caldwell House, Cataloochee, N.C., in 1937 (Great Smoky Mountains National Park).

keep boarders, 'cause they did keep boarders. And back then, we had drummers," noted Pearl Caldwell who lived in two such large houses during her adult life. (Both houses still survive; one is the circa 1900 Hiram Caldwell House in Cataloochee, now part of the Great Smoky Mountains National Park, the other is the circa 1906 Caldwell House in Maggie Valley.) Pearl Caldwell, who was born in a small log house but lived only in large houses after she married, added, "I never got to live in a little home like I'd like to." [31]

Tourism and summer visitation has been part of southwestern North Carolina's economy since soon after the opening of the Buncombe Turnpike. After the coming of the railroad, however, tourism vastly increased and summer visitation was no longer the province of the very wealthy who could afford to build grand summer homes. Some rural people who lived near railroad lines or main roads could profit from the influx of visitors. After their house in the Cowee Valley burned in 1914, Nora Moody's parents built a ten-room house with a center hallway. While her father farmed the river valley land, her mother, who placed advertisements in the *Atlanta Journal*, took in visitors who came by train from Georgia.[32] Traveling salesmen (drummers), individuals associated with the lumber industry, and school teachers also provided business to rural people with houses large enough to accommodate boarders. The few large homes of Cataloochee have attracted attention due to the seeming remoteness of the mountain community in northern Haywood County. Prior to the creation of the Great Smoky Mountains National Park, however, Cataloochee was located on a well-used road connecting North Carolina and Tennessee, and it attracted its share of summer visitors.[33] As Pearl Caldwell, a former Cataloochee resident, commented, "Everyone had people acoming fishing, they called it fishers, then. Everybody's looking for the fishers. And through the summer you had a pretty good job [boarding visitors]."[34]

Unlike the rural people who informally boarded travelers and welcomed strangers to their hearth, those who routinely boarded visitors for profit did create architectural barriers between themselves and their visitors. The hallway of the Hiram Caldwell House contained little more than a coat rack and some pictures on the wall. The formalization of relations between boarders and home owners was reflected in formalized spatial use. The boarders did not sleep among the family and a formal corridor provided access to rooms designated only for use by the boarders. Among those who profited from this formalized social relationship, the center hallway found acceptance as a formal passageway.

Oral and artifactual evidence suggests a history of ambivalence toward the center-passage plan in southwestern North Carolina. Only a minority seem to have accepted the central hall as a formal passageway. With the exception perhaps of the antebellum slaveholders who built I-houses as their first homes in the region and the later individuals who built large homes to board travelers, most builders of central-passage houses were in ambivalent social positions. The early pioneers who prospered and replaced their log homes with central-passage frame houses may have been reluctant to impose barriers of access into their homes against long-time neighbors. Post–Civil War builders of central-passage houses tended to be individuals of a slightly elevated status in the rural community, but they did not make up a separate class. Abram Evans was a rural storekeeper, Hugh Harvey Davidson, a sheriff and politician, and Julius McCoy was a schoolteacher. These builders were more likely than their rural neighbors to engage in "public" work. Individuals of this status, however, were also farmers, and in their everyday social lives they interacted with the mainstream rural society. Other builders of central-passage houses, such as Cornelius Gentile Price, farmed relatively good-sized, but not large, tracts of river valley land. Often these were portions of extensive holdings that had been divided by subsequent generations.

The underlying question is, of course, why these individuals chose the center-passage plan when it seemed to ill-fit their own patterns of spatial use. If they cared only for an imposing and symmetrical facade, other options were available. In Macon and Jackson counties, there are several surviving central chimney saddlebag houses that are a full two stories in height and have (or had) two-tiered porches with sawn-work trim. These houses have a four-bay facade with two front doors (such as the John Franklin Bryson House in Cullowhee) or have a three-bay facade with a central door (such as the nearby Bascom Bryson House).[35] These houses were very similar in appearance and size to the late nineteenth-century center-passage houses, and rural people did "count" these saddlebags as fine houses. "There was about three, or four, in the country built on that style, with the porch upstairs. The porch now that was something," commented Vestal Cochran of Nantahala, who remembers the large two-story houses in her section as always having a central chimney.[36] If the individuals who chose the center-passage plan did so for reasons of fashion, their reasons went be-

Figure 32. John Franklin Bryson House, two-story frame saddlebag (original porch removed), ca. 1890, Jackson County, N.C. (North Carolina Division of Archives and History, Western Office; photograph by Roger Manley).

yond the desire for an impressive facade, which could be achieved with a saddlebag house. They must have read some meaning in the center-passage plan itself.

The many functions of the dwelling make it impossible to isolate a single rule predicting the relationship between architectural form and social life. Surely, in folk building, the physical arrangement of space has some relationship to the actual social behavior that takes place within the dwelling's walls. Architectural form, however, is also believed to symbolize the structures of society.[37]

The concretization in architectural form of actual social behavior is not necessarily the same as the architectural symbolization of ideas about social organization. How then is a conflict between an ideal-

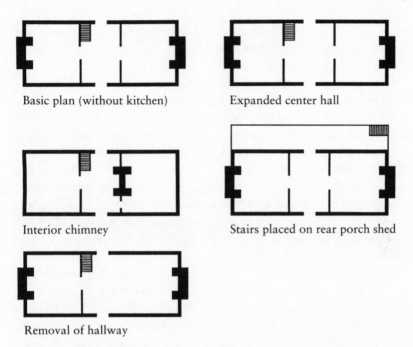

Basic plan (without kitchen)   Expanded center hall

Interior chimney   Stairs placed on rear porch shed

Removal of hallway

Figure 33. Variations of central-passage plan related to alternative spatial use

ized social milieu and actual social behavior manifested in architectural form? Is the center-passage I-house an artifact of ideas about social behavior or an artifact of social behavior itself, as expressed in spatial use?

The ambivalence toward the center-passage plan might well be correlated to the ambivalence the builders felt toward their social position in rural southwestern North Carolina. These were individuals of some ambition, but they were also rooted firmly in mainstream rural society. They accepted the central-passage plan, perhaps aware of its implications of formality and social control, but in actual use they did not depart from the norms of their rural society. Some builders perhaps were insightful enough to foresee the conflict rather than leave it simply to be worked out in later alterations and alternative uses. Tied to the norms of rural society, these individuals softened the implications of the plan by permitting immediate access into the social core of their house or by utilizing the formal space of the central passage.

Outwardly, the builders of central-passage houses communicated a sense of high status with their choice of house type. Inwardly, many conformed to the norms of the community's traditional patterns of spatial use. Builders, or subsequent users, conceptually or physically manipulated an incompatible house form to achieve this conformity. In choice of house type the builder projected a public image, but the builder and occupants of the house were unwilling to jeopardize their part in the intimacy of the community. Viewing the center-passage house, the outsider might recognize the status of the owner, but friends and neighbors on entering the house found comfortably familiar patterns of social interaction.[38]

Narratives about the experience of the central-passage dwelling in southwestern North Carolina demonstrate that systems of spatial use might conflict with architectural form. We know this to be true in cases of displaced persons—African slaves who found themselves in Anglo-American folk houses, foreign immigrants in urban America.[39] In modern society as well, we know of many people who, having little control over their architectural environment, subvert intended use in their domestic spatial patterns. The important difference is that in southwestern North Carolina there was a folk building tradition in which the individuals had considerable control over the nature of their dwellings. The user was usually the designer, if not the builder, of the home. The conflict between spatial use and architectural form was not rooted in the difference between builder and user but in the dwelling's unresolved multiplicity of functions. The builders of center-passage houses did not have architectural form imposed on them by an outside dominant culture, but, we might suspect, the plan was imposed by the nature of their own aspirations. While appeasing these aspirations in form, in use they were confined by the norms of their neighbors and family.

CHAPTER FIVE

Abandonment and the "Old Homeplace"

The meaning of the house is not found in its physical aspects alone. The idea of "home" is largely independent of the form the dwelling takes. The physical shell only contains the home, or represents the memory of a home of the past. For many, it is a past home, particularly the home of one's childhood, that has the greatest emotional meaning. The present house, although "home," is often taken for granted. In southwestern North Carolina, unless you are one of the few who still lives in their childhood home (or you are still a child), the homeplace is not your present house. Speaking of her house, Willa Mae Pressley, perhaps more optimistic about the continuation of tradition than some of her neighbors, commented, "Each generation has its own old homeplace. So hopefully, this will be my children's old homeplace."[1] The adjective "old" is often automatically appended to "homeplace."

On the surface the rural people of southwestern North Carolina appear to place little value on old houses. For a people known for their retention of intangible cultural traditions, they have not treated their architectural heritage well.[2] In many areas, one sees little architectural evidence of the nineteenth century, and structures that predate the Civil War are rare. Still, empty houses litter the rural landscape. Frequently these houses, which are "too old to live in," are not more than sixty or seventy years old. Houses that have been officially enshrined as "significant" are, for the most part, monuments to the attraction of the region's physical beauty and mild climate to wealthy intruders. George Vanderbilt's testament to personal wealth, Biltmore House, or the far-from-modest summer homes of wealthy lowlanders at Flat Rock, have little personal significance to the average rural dweller.

Yet, despite the widespread abandonment and destruction of old houses in southwestern North Carolina, many individuals speak of the old homeplace with tears in their eyes. How does one reconcile the emotional meaning people find in the idea of the homeplace with willful abandonment and destruction? One might attribute the fate of old houses in the region to the social and economic change imposed upon the region in the early to mid-twentieth century. As rural life became less tenable, many sold out to forestry interests, and with the eventual collapse of the timber boom, some left the region in search of other "public work."[3] Others were forcibly removed as a result of the creation of the Tennessee Valley Authority and the Great Smoky Mountains National Park.[4] During this period a long-held building tradition finally met its demise, and with it went a traditional aesthetic system. Many of the individuals who remain in the country actively prefer new houses (including prefab and mobile homes) to old houses. Houses of sixty or seventy years are old, not chronologically, but in the aesthetic they represent. Perhaps the emotion expressed about the homeplace is merely the nostalgia or sentimentality that accompanies change. Ambivalence is not surprising under such circumstances. While social and economic change may be one reason for the abandonment and destruction of old houses, these factors need to be examined closely. For instance, outmigration and the conversion of farm land to non-agricultural uses account for relatively few of the empty houses still standing. In cases where whole families moved out, and the farms ceased to be farms, the structures usually disappeared with the people. Buildings were moved, salvaged for materials, or simply destroyed.[5]

In most cases, where old houses are still standing, family members live nearby. The houses are not truly abandoned; people keep an eye on them from a trailer next door, a ranch house across the road, or a mod-

Figure 34. Modern ranch house above empty homeplace, Cherokee County, N.C. (North Carolina Division of Archives and History, Western Office; photograph by the author).

ern home in town. It is often to the frustration of rural preservationists that the owners of these houses refuse to sell, rent, or sometimes even maintain, empty houses.[6] The attitude of the owners, however, is not simple rural obstinacy. These empty houses have a function, a social and symbolic role in the life of the former inhabitants. Understanding the role of these empty houses makes apparent the fact that contemporary attitudes toward old houses are rooted in tradition, not in the rejection of tradition.

In order to understand the meaning of old houses, one must first understand the use of the term "homeplace." In southwestern North Carolina, homeplace generally does not refer to the family's property. It is not the whole spread of land, Arvel Greene explained, just "the immediate area where the old house was, where they all lived and was brought up, they just called that the old homeplace."[7] Although "homeplace" may include the area surrounding the house, it is seldom used as an equivalent to "house and yard." The meaning is not a simple geographic designation.[8] "Homeplace" under certain circumstances, however, may refer to the site of the house. Individuals may visit the "old homeplace" although the structure itself is gone.

When asked if the homeplace is the house or the land, Willa Mae Pressley responded, "I think maybe your memories, or mine, are more of the house. You know, and just close around the house, not the other property. You can remember, like back roaming around all over the hills and all that, but I think the house has more meaning."[9] The homeplace is a home of the past, not the present; a place that has meaning. "People called it the homeplace. Talk about it, like when you're talking about my old home, where I was raised. We'd call it the homeplace" (Oma Jenkins).[10]

Arvel Greene, Willa Mae Pressley, and others noted that the homeplace changed with every generation. Your parents' homeplace, your homeplace, and your children's homeplace are not necessarily the same thing. The homeplace is not a symbol of the distant past or of many generations of a single family. Rather, it is a symbol of the individual's own past and the individual's immediate family. That the homeplace tended to change with each generation also reflects the patterns of rural building. Only a minority of rural folk dwellings were lived in by more than one or two consecutive generations of a family.

The destruction and replacement of rural dwellings in southwestern North Carolina was not solely a twentieth-century phenomenon. The concept of homeplace is tied to patterns of rebuilding. The widespread preference for small houses made it more likely that each generation would build new houses rather than pass a home on as a cherished treasure. Those who used log construction and participated in cooperative building could build a house with little cash outlay. Therefore, this basic type of folk housing was accessible to almost anyone in the rural community.

The rebuilding that went on between generations was not necessarily the result of improving family fortunes or changes in stylistic preferences.[11] Of course, in some cases, particularly in the river valleys, prosperity resulted in a change in the family's type of house, as in the case of Robert Orr, who built his frame I-house downriver from his father's log saddlebag "mansion." Generally, however, the basically conservative nature of rural building in southwestern North Carolina led to subsequent generations building relatively similar small rural houses. Ernest Justus remembered several generations of building by his family on a single piece of land. John Justus acquired the family property in Upward, Henderson County, in 1825 and built a small log house. A generation later W. D. Justus built a similar size frame house, and in 1905 his son, Frank Justus, built a one-story center-passage house. Frank Justus's sons, Ernest and Drayton, built new houses in the mid-twentieth century.[12] This sequence shows a progressive pattern of rebuilding by a well-off rural family, but through the early twentieth century all the houses were moderately small traditional plan dwellings. Other families simply built generation after generation of single pen log houses.

In cases where a house was continuously lived in by several generations, the house itself was often subject to continual alteration. Old houses became ells for newer houses; old ells were torn down and replaced.[13] Bass Hyatt's grandfather, H. H. Davidson, bought a farm in Brasstown, Clay County, from Bob Bell after the Civil War. The house then consisted of a log house with a log kitchen. Davidson tore down the kitchen and made the rest of the house an ell for a new single-story center-passage frame house. Hyatt's family tore down the log ell and replaced it with a "boxed house." Later, Hyatt and his brother tore down that ell and built a new two-story frame house, making the old single-story center-passage house a rear ell to it.[14]

The families who occupied the larger center-passage houses were probably more successful in passing the house down to more than one

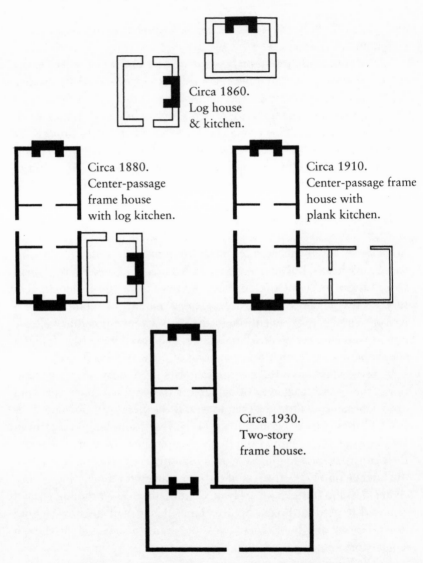

Circa 1860.
Log house
& kitchen.

Circa 1880.
Center-passage
frame house
with log kitchen.

Circa 1910.
Center-passage frame
house with
plank kitchen.

Circa 1930.
Two-story
frame house.

Figure 35. Evolution of the Davidson-Hyatt homestead, Brasstown, N.C.

or two generations. Both of the individuals interviewed who lived in relatively unaltered nineteenth-century dwellings lived in substantial frame center-passage houses. Katherine Porter resided in her great-great-grandfather Hall's two-story I-house; Frances Bryson, in a two-story house built by her husband's grandfather.[15] Still, even the more substantial houses seem to have been subject to the vagaries of local inheritance patterns and the widespread preference for rebuilding. French Haynes of Haywood County recalled that her father tore down a large brick house in about 1897, replacing it with a center-passage frame house. That house was, in turn, replaced in 1928 after an active life of only thirty-one years. At about the same time the home of French Haynes's grandfather, also a center-passage house, was destroyed. "At that time, it was an old, old house. It was at least seventy-five years old," Miss Haynes commented.[16] In some areas evidence of the pre–Civil War planter class has almost completely disappeared. Despite the presence of several prominent slaveholding families, none of the antebellum "plantation" houses in Cherokee County survive, except the McCombs House, which was so extensively altered in the 1920s that little of the original architectural fabric is apparent.[17]

Rebuilding took place not only between generations but also within a single generation. Several individuals interviewed recalled moving once or even twice to new houses on the same property during their childhood.[18] Again, this was not just an early twentieth-century phenomenon. According to R. O. Wilson, his grandfather built a single-room log house after the Civil War. Several years later he built a slightly larger log house: "It was one big long room, and they may have partitioned it." The older house became a detached kitchen. Finally, in about 1898 his grandfather built a frame saddlebag house. "They built it just above the old log house, and tore the old log structure down. Probably burned it for firewood, I guess."[19] Not all the rebuildings were substantial improvements. Robert Blanton's family in Brush Creek, Swain County, moved intermittently from one single pen log house to another until in 1918 they built a third log home.[20]

The reasons for a preference for rebuilding are complex, particularly in light of a very conservative building tradition. Other scholars have attempted to grapple with the question of architectural impermanence and the issue of why, in choosing to rebuild, an individual would opt for newer, but not necessarily better, housing. It has been proposed that the building of impermanent earthfast dwellings in the seventeenth-century Chesapeake colonies was due, in part, to the social instability that resulted from a high mortality rate and an economic reliance on the fluctuating tobacco market. These factors rendered each generation as homesteaders.[21]

While the situation was less dire in nineteenth-century southwestern North Carolina, a prolonged period of "homesteading" also characterized this region. The area had barely emerged from a pioneer economy when the Civil War, and its punishing ramifications, squashed much hope of agricultural prosperity. The average mountain farmer of the nineteenth century could probably not count on leaving the world with much more than he entered it. Rather than bequeathing his family a fine home, he left them a building technology and a tradition of cooperative building that would provide his heirs with new houses. Cooperative building in turn reinforced the continued construction of small, traditional dwellings. The individual who relied on the voluntary efforts of neighbors in constructing a house was likely to readily accede to the building norms of the community. In many families each generation started anew with small houses that could be added to or replaced. An individual might even have the option of building two or three houses during his or her lifetime.

Nineteenth-century southwestern North Carolina differed from the Chesapeake colonies of two centuries before in that the architecture was not, in itself, physically impermanent. Impermanence lay in its use, not in its technology. In fact, active use of a dwelling often ended before its physical condition warranted. Houses sometimes deteriorated quickly because they were left empty, not because they were badly built. As many former inhabitants will testify, many nineteenth-century log dwellings were "built to last";[22] but, even the most substantial dwellings (such as French Haynes's grandfather's house) were thought of as "old, old" by the age of seventy-five. The desire to rebuild rather than retain dwellings seems to have been ingrained in the attitudes of individuals across a broad spectrum of rural society. Instead of dire poverty, the abandonment of still habitable dwellings suggests a degree of wastefulness.

Except for the early pioneer era, the building of physically impermanent architecture was not prevalent until after 1900, when many rural builders began to eschew the use of hewn logs for "pole" or "plank" construction.[23] Although this might be interpreted as a degeneracy of the folk tradition, the builders of pole (unhewn log) and plank (vertical board) houses were often individuals who were desperately clinging to their rural lifestyles. Among these people the preference was still for small, traditional plan houses that could be built by the individual with the help of family or neighbors. As individuals found it necessary to seek "public work," however, people simply had less time to spare for building houses. While other aspects of traditional building were maintained, permanence was sacrificed. Time was no longer taken to hew logs square.[24] Eventually, as sawmills were increasingly found in even the remotest communities, people built with rough sawn planks.[25] "You could go and buy lumber at some of these sawmills, they's in every cove, two or three down through this country. You could buy lumber to put you up a four room house, for about thirty-five or forty dollar. . . . There'd be a crowd, be a bunch of people right in the country, they'd just come automatically, help you throw your house right up," Grady Carringer explained. Lumber was put up green: "You'd be in a hurry to have a house built."[26]

The physical impermanence of frameless plank houses did not seem to concern the builders who were already conditioned to think of houses as replaceable.[27] Despite their shortcomings, boxed houses were faster to build than log homes, and some individuals aesthetically preferred them to log as they were perceived to be modern. Individuals who grew up in frame houses were apt to be more critical. Jessie Frazier's father used boxed construction in building houses to rent to individuals employed in the timber industry, Mrs. Frazier explained, because

Figure 36. "Old Bennett Boxed House," Little Cataloochee, N.C., in 1937 (Great Smoky Mountains National Park).

"he wasn't building them to stay there forever."[28] (The timber industry may have been responsible for introducing boxed housing to the region. However, this impermanent form of building, which made sense in the context of the timber camp, was quickly adopted for use in rural farmsteads.) Another critic, Jim Neal, argued that a boxed house "wouldn't hold together," giving its life-span as approximately forty or fifty years. "It would be cheaper in the long run [to build a boxed house], but it wouldn't be as good. But you know a fellow builds a house, he generally spends his lifetime in it, he just about spends a lifetime."[29] Jim Neal's criticism is interesting because it articulates the ideal from which the boxed house diverged. He does not argue that a man should build a house which he can pass on to his heirs, but rather he implies that a house should at least last the lifetime of its builder.[30] The typical life-span of the dwelling, and hence the homeplace, was a single generation.

Inheritance patterns also shaped patterns of rebuilding. The very small size of most rural houses largely precluded the housing of ex-tended families under a single roof. While a grown son with his own family might live with his parents, this was usually only after his sib-lings had left home and was far more common when only one parent was surviving. Nor was the builder likely to turn over his household to an adult child during his lifetime (unlike, for instance, traditional pat-terns among Pennsylvania Germans where the home would be turned over to a child upon his adulthood and a smaller "grossvater" house might be built for an aging parent). On the death of the builder, his widow would be accorded dower's rights to the house. "The mother always keeps the homeplace," Lucy Hyatt explained.[31] Zena Bennett commented that the wife usually "just gets a widow's dower, she gets to stay at the homeplace as long as she lives. Then the children get equal, everything equal."[32]

The fact that the homeplace remained the property of the builder or his widow during his or her lifetime often made the intergenerational transfer of ownership difficult. Inheritance of land, on the other hand, was basically egalitarian. The individuals interviewed uniformly agreed that land was ideally divided equally between the male heirs, or more commonly, between all the male and female children. This pattern had several important ramifications. The continual dividing of land made it difficult for families to keep large tracts of land intact and impeded the development of a stable rural elite. Outmigration eased the burden somewhat. As Larry Gunter noted, "Some of them would wander off to other country, you know, and they didn't want nothing back here. They'd get to be doing well. But they would generally divide it up."[33] (Outmigration was a significant factor in the early twentieth century, but even during the nineteenth century it was not uncommon for a family member to be lured off to seek his fortune in California, Texas, or elsewhere.) The fact that tracts of land got smaller and smaller, that a

Figure 37. Inheritance of land was basically egalitarian. The Yarborough family, early twentieth century. Zena Yarborough Bennett is in second row, second from the right.

married couple might stand to inherit land from either his or her family, and that some of the heirs might choose to leave the area altogether led to a great deal of selling of land among the various heirs.[34] Those who chose to stay would usually build a new house on their own land near the homeplace. While residence patterns probably favored settling near the husband's homeplace, this was not invariably the pattern. Lolita Dean, for instance, reported that her father originally built a house near his family but then relocated to a tract of land adjacent to his wife's parents' place.[35]

The passing on of the homeplace disturbed the basically egalitarian division of property. Several rules existed as to who was to inherit the home, most accommodating the long tenure of the parents at the homeplace. The question "Who usually inherited the homeplace?" elicited a variety of responses: "The youngest son" (Nanny Sorrells).[36] "Lot of times, now, in several instances, they'd let the property go to the one that takes care of them" (Minnie McDonald).[37] "The baby one in the family always got the home" (Mary Messer).[38] "Youngest one of them boys" (Jim Neal).[39] "The one that stayed there the longest" (Bessie Tilley).[40] "It was just how ever the old man and woman wanted to will it off or give it off. There was no rule" (Arvel Greene).[41]

Generally, the responses were split between preference for the youngest child (or youngest boy) and the last at home (or the one who took care of the parents the longest). Frequently, but not always, this was the same child. A minority believed that there simply was no standard rule. Different rules or interpretations might even exist within the same family. Oma Jenkins, for instance, believed that there was no rule, but generally, parents might will the homeplace to a child on condition that he take care of them. Mrs. Jenkins's daughter, however, noted that in her father's community, the house usually went to the youngest: "It depended on what creek you lived on, I think, and what the custom was."[42] Anna Collett and her husband fell victim to differing interpretations of inheritance rules: "The parents said in the beginning that the one that stayed with them the longest, wanted them to have the homeplace. So, my husband and me, we stayed with them the longest. But then the family decided that youngest wanted the homeplace." The youngest, however, had already built a new house. "The rest of the family wanted the youngest boy to have the homeplace so we just exchanged houses."[43]

Some individuals cited general rules for inheritance of the homeplace but noted their own family deviated from the pattern. Monroe Ledford, for instance, said, "It didn't happen in our family like that, but I guess the ones that took care of the parents mostly got the home."[44] French Haynes recalled that the youngest son usually inherited the home but then cited two cases in her own family where the house went to an unmarried daughter.[45] In some instances the homeplace simply remained undivided property. In obtaining ownership information during the course of county surveys, I was told on several occasions that a rural dwelling was owned "by the heirs."[46] Three of the individuals interviewed owned, or had owned, the homeplace only by virtue of buying out the other heirs.[47]

The fact that the house usually remained in the possession of the parents until both their deaths enhanced the probability that the dwelling would not be actively used for more than one or two generations. In many instances, by the time of both parents' deaths, the youngest child had already elected to build his or her own house and did not care to move back into the old house. On the other hand, the preference for the house to go to the last at home highly increased the possibility that the house would be inherited by an unmarried child. (Some married couples, however, did move in with parents and in-laws in order to be the last at home.)

The cultural priority placed on maintaining the homeplace for both or one of the parents until their deaths did not resolve the problems of inheritance. The abandonment of old dwellings would lead one to think that no one cared to own the old homeplace. This was definitely not the case. Inheritance of the homeplace was imbued with a great deal of emotional significance and potential conflict. Stories about family problems centering on the inheritance of the homeplace abound. Several individuals interviewed refused to talk about inheritance of their homeplace on tape. Others expressed bitterness about who inherited the home or what the heir chose to do with it. Stories about conflict over inheritance have made their way into the narrative tradition. Zena Bennett told an amusing story about two brothers bitterly quarreling over ownership of the homeplace (the moral of which was that it is better to settle conflicts within the family than employ lawyers).[48] During the course of my first survey one individual told me that so many rural houses were empty because families could not decide who was to inherit them. Taking the comment to be humorous, I did not, at first, realize that there was some truth in it.

The nature of the symbolic significance of the homeplace may be seen as a product of patterns of rebuilding reinforced by inheritance patterns.

Because the house often did not get passed through several generations it could only be a symbol of the immediate family and recent past. The depth of conflict about inheritance of the homeplace, however, suggests that the opposite is also true. The symbolic significance of the home actively reinforced patterns of inheritance and rebuilding.

While the parents were still alive, the homeplace could function symbolically without conflict. As the children "went to housekeeping," the homeplace became an important symbol of the family and childhood left behind. The passing on of the house to a single sibling introduced a potential conflict in the role of the house. Was the dwelling *our* homeplace or *their* house? In some families the conflict was eased if the sibling continued to welcome his or her brothers and sisters back and treated the house as if it was their home as well. Leslie Ward recalled, "My daddy always said he wanted me to have the homeplace, 'cause I was the last to marry. Of all the bunch of children I was the last to marry. And I stayed here for twelve year after he died, you know, my mother lived here with us. . . . But [my brothers and sisters] all come back when they was aliving. It felt like home to them you know. Have dinners, get together, have a good time."[49] A similar case was cited by Robert Blanton: "That's the homeplace down there on Brush Creek. And we, after they all got scattered off, why at least for a year or two there, we had a regular family reunion. And they'd come down there to the old place. And they all sold out their share after our mother died, except me. And I kept what I had there. And they would come back to the old place and have a reunion."[50] Other families were less successful in easing the tension over a sibling living at the homeplace. It not only caused resentment among those who did not inherit the house but also was a burden for those who did. Bessie Tilley and her husband inherited his family's homeplace: "We stayed here the longest, and when the land was divided, they give us the homeplace. . . . Lawrence was the baby one. [But it was] just because we stayed here the longest." Asked what people meant by the homeplace, Mrs. Tilley responded, "Where they were raised." Then she added in a good-natured manner: "And it's not a good place. I'll give you a little piece of advice. Don't ever stay at the homeplace if you can help it. If you marry, are you married? Well it's a gathering place for all the relatives. It's hard on you. I found that out." [51]

Some inheritance patterns tried to deal with the problem. The preference for the house to go to an unmarried sibling was particularly effective. The unmarried sibling might then assume a surrogate parent role by maintaining the house and welcoming the brothers and sisters "home." The unmarried sibling posed less of a threat to the house's symbolic role and would not, in turn, pass the house on to the next generation. Keeping the house as jointly owned, undivided property also attempted to deal with the problem of inheritance of the homeplace by keeping the house under the control of the extended family. If an unmarried sibling continued to live at the homeplace, often the house was jointly owned by the heirs.

In many cases the homeplace functioned most effectively as a symbol when it was simply not lived in. An empty house is a potent symbol of the past. The house is also a better symbol of the family who once lived there if another family has not taken up residence. One child may own or be designated to maintain the homeplace, but it still functions as *our* home. For this reason many families keep old houses empty but do not truly abandon them. The house does have a use. Its function as a symbol, however, has taken precedence over its functions as a shelter or container of social activity.

The "abandonment" of the homeplace is, in part, another result of conflict in the multiple functions of the dwelling. The builder alone cannot possibly resolve all functional conflict. No simple hierarchy guides the builder's design decisions nor can the builder foresee the functional priorities of the users. And most relevant to the case of the homeplace, the functional roles of the house may change over the life history of the structure. Functional conflicts do cause alteration and abandonment of structures. In the case of the homeplace, however, "abandonment" is actually a change in functional priority ascribed to the house. In the conflict between the house as shelter, social container, or symbol, the symbolic role has won.

Understanding the abandonment of the homeplace as a product of functional conflict explains why some rural western North Carolinians keep empty houses on their property, refusing to sell or rent them. The house has meaning, even if it does not seem to be actively used. This explanation, however, does not explain the destruction or neglect of old houses in the region. A closer examination of the nature of the role of the old homeplace provides some of the answers.

In rural southwestern North Carolina, structures are rarely valued simply for the virtue of being old. There are relatively few architectural monuments of the collective history of region, county, or community. Rural communities, in fact, tended to have few public buildings. Post offices were frequently located in private homes, and a single structure sometimes served as the church for more than one denomination and occasionally doubled as the school and local meeting hall. While the churches were an important focal point in many rural communities, the structures themselves seemed subject to the same preference for rebuilding as did dwellings. Potentially, dwellings carried the strongest symbolic weight of any rural structures. However, houses that did not have the role of homeplace tended to be symbolically weak. As we have seen, the "homeplace" frequently changes with every generation, making it a symbol of the immediate family rather than of generations past. The valuation of the homeplace as a symbol of the immediate family tends to strip older houses of a potential symbolic significance. If several old houses manage to survive on a property, it is the younger and not the older structures that have the most meaning. One does not value the homeplace of one's parents or grandparents to the degree one values one's own homeplace. As a generation of a family passes away, their homeplace quickly loses its meaning. Beyond a certain point, the symbolic significance of an old dwelling decreases, rather than increases, with age.

The rebuilding that takes place within a generation also devalues older structures. If a family moves to a new house on the same property, it is the newer and not the older structure that usually becomes the homeplace. In Robert Blanton's family it was the new log house begun in 1918, and not the two older log houses, that became the homeplace.

The older houses were destroyed.[52] Oma Jenkins's father replaced their log house with a "lumber" house in 1904, when she was six years old. Leslie Ward's father replaced the log home he had built himself with a large frame house in 1909, the year Mrs. Ward was born. Both women remember using the log homes as playhouses when they were young. And both houses met the same fate. "Best I remember, [my father] just tore it down and burned it for stovewood," Mrs. Jenkins recalled.[53] Mrs. Ward remembered, "We just tore it down and burnt the logs for wood."[54] Often, unless the old house was put to a practical purpose, such as conversion to a barn or kitchen, it was simply destroyed after the replacement house was finished. Individuals who acquired property with structures already built also felt no compunction about destroying still-habitable dwellings in favor of new houses.

In recent years attitudes about old houses have begun to change among older people in southwestern North Carolina as they begin to grow nostalgic for a way of life that has passed. Many have also been affected by the recent popular romanticizing about rural Appalachian life. The change in attitude has generally not resulted in a move toward rural preservation, but it has translated into regret over former actions. Most of this sentiment focuses on log houses. Zena Bennett said that it never even occurred to her and her husband to save the log house that was on the property they bought in the Iotla community of Macon County. Initially, they thought about only saving a three-room frame addition to the log house, but they were persuaded otherwise by neighbors. "Then, they advised us to build a new house, while we built. Build on an old house, you always have an old house, so we decided to build a new house." Mrs. Bennett now regrets that they did not keep the log house, instead of burning it for firewood.[55] Essie Moore and her husband tore down her great-grandfather's log house, after they acquired the tract of land it was on, and built a new house instead. Now, Mrs. Moore regrets the decision: "I don't see why we didn't restore it in place of this. Them logs was good. We'd have something if we done that. It was a huge house, too."[56] Relatively few rural people even now actually want to live in an old log house, although many would not mind having one decorate their property. Even the most modern and pragmatic realize now that the log houses they chose to destroy were worth more than firewood.

Prior to this recent rise in sentimentality about log houses, emotion about old houses focused almost solely on the homeplace, rendering other old dwellings relatively meaningless. The degree of symbolic value placed on the homeplace, however, does not necessarily translate into physical maintenance of the structure. While most people expressed very similar sentiments about the homeplace, there was a high degree of variability in how the homeplace was physically treated.

In some cases the old homeplace takes on a new social role even if it was not lived in. While family might gather at a homeplace lived in by a sibling, an empty homeplace could also serve as a site for family reunions. Some people specifically maintain a home for this purpose. Eula Bryson of Cowee, Macon County, bought her homeplace from the other heirs. The frame house, built in 1907 and expanded in 1910, replaced a log house that was torn down when the frame house was built. Although Mrs. Bryson does not live in the house, it is beautifully maintained. "We still have our reunion there at the old homeplace every year. There was almost a hundred there this year," Mrs. Bryson explained. She took it as her role to provide a place for the family to gather.[57]

Even if a house does not have a specific role, some individuals carefully preserve their home. One gentleman took me through his homeplace, a relatively small frame house that stood across the road from his modern ranch house. The inside, still furnished, was clean and dusted; the outside, freshly painted. The family even took care to mow and maintain the yard.[58]

The choice of carefully maintaining an unlived-in homeplace is more often the exception rather than the rule. Despite the emotion imbued in the homeplace, many people do not find it inappropriate to let nature take its course. A structure may weather, or begin to lean, or become overgrown with weeds, but it is still the homeplace. It is treated with respect, but many people do not feel compelled to make an old building look new. After all, it is a symbol of the past. Even more startling is

Figure 38. Homeplace, empty but still furnished and well maintained. W. J. Martin House, ca. 1905, Cherokee County, N.C. (North Carolina Division of Archives and History, Western Office; photograph by the author).

Figure 39. Homeplace converted first to a kitchen and then to a barn. Surry Ann Jones House, Henderson County, N.C. (North Carolina Division of Archives and History, Western Office; photograph by the author).

the fact that although the roles of homeplace and dwelling may conflict, many people are willing to give the old homeplace additional non-social functions. A homeplace may double as a barn for the housing of live-stock or the storage of hay or farm equipment, or it may serve as a "junk house" for miscellaneous possessions. These functions would seem to devalue the meaning of the homeplace, but this is not necessarily the case. It is a testament to the complexity of the house that such diverse functions, if not in conflict, can coexist.[59] An individual may use the house for such practical purposes because the meaning of the home is not to be found in the physical structure itself.

The detachment of the meaning of the homeplace from the physical structure is, at the most extreme, represented by those who make pil-grimages to empty house sites. Eller Garrett's father sold their farm at the head of Beaverdam in Cherokee County to the federal government and moved to Georgia. The house where Mrs. Garrett had grown up was torn down, but "we go back up there every time we get a chance. My baby sister, she was born and raised after they left this country. And every time she can, maybe once a year or something, they'll come back, her and her husband, and we'll go up to dad's old place. We call it the homeplace, 'we got to go back to the homeplace.' "[60] Another woman from Cherokee County wept when she described going back to the site of the house where she was raised: "I went over there a year or two ago. And, no, it was last summer, I went over with my nieces and I said, 'I'm going out yonder where Glenn was born and look the place over.' Well, I went on out there; and, seemed like the memories poured out. Oh mercy. Seemèd like they just come meeting me."[61] So strong was the memory that the woman was moved to tears describing her visit.

In these instances, the homeplace literally is a place. But it is not the property or the landscape, any more than it is the physical structure, that is important. The empty house site, or the empty house, is a symbol of the experience, or memories of the experience, of home. The power of the homeplace lies in its ability to evoke these memories.

People who no longer have physical access to their homeplace seek solace in the power of narrative. Through their stories people may still travel home. Many of the narratives I heard had been polished over the years, as people studied on their pasts and gave shape to their experiences. For the people who told them, the stories, too, were precious symbols of home. For scholars these stories are also artifacts. While many times I crossed snaky fields in high boots and crept gingerly across rotting porches to inspect old structures, the entrance to the homeplace, I found, was through these oral narratives.

CONCLUSION

In a region such as southwestern North Carolina where there is little popular support for rural preservation, traditional dwellings are rapidly disappearing from the rural landscape. In our efforts to document these structures before they vanish, however, we have neglected an even more fragile category of evidence, the memory of the experience of the house. If we only focus on tangible evidence, even the most comprehensive survey is limited in what it is capable of revealing about the meaning of the folk dwelling. Nor will a cursory use of oral history add much to our knowledge, if it is limited only to the facts of building and ownership of extant structures.

Oral history may be used to reconstruct the totality of an architectural environment.[1] This reconstruction is important when the variable survivability of structures skews the objective nature of architectural evidence. It is particularly crucial where we have failed to recognize architectural impermanence as a factor. Of the early twentieth-century rural dwellings of southwestern North Carolina, the most and the least traditional have survived. Structures representative of the rural norm have largely disappeared. Architectural histories based only on the evidence of extant structures are likely to give a distorted view of the past.

Oral testimony, however, is more than an artifact of an artifact. While it provides a means to more accurately reconstruct the tangible evidence of the past, it is also direct evidence in itself. An individual may use verbal means to give form to the intangible aspects of architectural experience that are incompletely manifested in physical form. Oral testimony may be the best evidence available of these intangibles. The complexities of use and meaning that frustrate the student of the artifact may be reexamined in the light of the evidence of oral testimony.

Scholars who deal with tangible evidence, whether it be documentary or artifactual, often express skepticism about oral evidence. Of course, memories falter, people lie. But in dealing with more than a few informants, ascertaining the truthfulness of the testimony is one of the easier aspects of the interpretation of oral evidence. (Lack of truthfulness, in fact, is often as revealing as the truth.) The greater problem is one faced by all students of culture searching for patterns, systems, and rules. How does one deal with the incredible diversity of individual experience? The challenge in using oral evidence to understand shared aspects of architectural use and meaning is not to lose sight of the individual nature of architectural experience.

The limits of usefulness of oral testimony in understanding aspects of architectural use and meaning are set by the ability of the individual to articulate, on some level, his or her experience. Of course, oral testimony, like other categories of evidence, must be interpreted, but oral testimony is of little use in understanding a subject that the informants are unwilling or unable to talk about. In order to avoid making too much of too little, we need to accept that oral testimony is useful in understanding some, but not all, aspects of the intangible nature of architecture. The choice to focus on spatial use and the meaning of the homeplace in this study was guided, in part, by the nature of the information obtained in the oral interviews. This study hardly exhausts the subject of architectural use and meaning in southwestern North Carolina. Alternative interviewing strategies might, in fact, clarify other aspects of architectural use in the region.

In future studies of architectural use the unit of study must be carefully examined. Several folklorists using ethnographic observation or oral history to study architecture have demonstrated that the commu-

Figure 40. With increased development, traditional dwellings are disappearing from the landscape (Photograph by the author).

nity can be an effective unit of analysis.[2] In some instances, however, practical considerations may prevent community study from being a useful tool. As in this study, there may simply not be enough informants from a single community to provide perspective on a crucial time period still accessible by oral history. Also, while community study provides a better way of reconstructing the totality of an architectural environment, it may be less reliable if broader regional patterns are of interest. A single community may be no more representative of a region than a single individual is representative of a community. In southwestern North Carolina, norms varied considerably between rural communities. By 1900, for instance, frame houses were common in the rural community of Cowee along the Little Tennessee River.[3] Not more than twenty miles away in the communities of Alarka and Brush Creek in

Swain County, log was the norm through the 1920s.[4] These communities represented two extremes, for the majority of individuals interviewed reported a preponderance of plank structures with a smaller
number of either log or frame buildings. Choosing a relatively well-
defined region permits some understanding of this subregional diversity.
The informants, however, spoke primarily of individual experience; the
most difficult facet of analysis was the judgment of what aspects of their
experience were shared by the community or the region as a whole.

Although comparative data on architectural use and meaning is still
relatively sparse, that which is available is certainly suggestive of the
widespread temporal and geographic distribution of certain spatial patterns. Spatial use in southwestern North Carolina is probably charac-
teristic of the broader regional patterns of Southern Appalachia or the
Upland South as a whole.[5] There may also be similarities with Anglo-
American and African-American spatial patterns in the folk houses in
some parts of the Lowland South.[6] The evidence also suggests that similar spatial patterns were associated with related architectural forms,
temporally or geographically distant from late nineteenth- and early
twentieth-century southwestern North Carolina.[7] The conservative retention of traditional spatial patterns, however, should not be attributed
solely to the geographical isolation of Southern Appalachia. Rather,
conclusions about spatial change should consider social and cultural,
as well as temporal, factors. Some American vernacular architecture research still tends to have a relatively elite bias. More broad-based studies
of spatial use in nineteenth-century America might reveal far more conservative patterns of use than is indicated by the current literature on
the subject.[8]

This study can only begin to suggest the possibilities for understanding architectural use and meaning through oral testimony. While the
main goal was to better understand the experiential aspects of folk
architecture, the conclusions reached also have implications for artifactual research. The dwelling is often chosen as a premiere historical artifact because of its universality and its complexity.[9] Shelter is essential
and the act of dwelling, basic to human existence. The house not only

fulfills an essential physical function, the protection of the inhabitant from the environment, but also has well-developed social and symbolic functions. The house is "home," the center of family life. It is a container of social activity and a cultural symbol. The social and symbolic functions of the house are not discrete entities, however. For instance, the study of spatial use provides insight into both the social and symbolic nature of the dwelling. Spatial use represents a system of culturally transmitted ideas, including ideas about both the nature of space and the nature of social relationships. Domestic space may be used symbolically to represent aspects of the social structure. Spatial use, however, is also representative of the patterns of actual social behavior.[10]

The multiplicity of functions of the dwelling, while contributing to the richness of the house as an artifact, also poses problems for the interpreter. Are certain physical attributes of structure meant to satisfy physical, social, or symbolic needs? Although some sort of integration of functions is necessary, the builder or designer is often faced with basic functional conflict. For instance, environmental demands on design may be quite different from social demands. While some scholars have noted the tendency for social concerns to dominate environmental ones in folk building, the builder is not guided by any simple hierarchy of functions.[11] Nor does the builder necessarily resolve all functional conflict that may be manifested later in conflicts between use and form. In order to understand the functional complexity of the dwelling, one must examine architectural use as well as the building process.

House form has been taken as an important artifact of spatial ideas and use. Still, the interpreter of the artifact must be cautious, as evidence suggests a degree of independence in spatial use and form. John Vlach rests his argument for the African antecedents of the shotgun house largely on the continuity of spatial preference rather than on the more tenuous continuity of physical form. "Held in the unconscious mind these preferences proved less malleable than the physical dimension of architecture. The social pattern that accompanies the American shotgun house is ostensibly more African than the house itself."[12] It has also been hypothesized that the slaves of lowland South Carolina maintained

African spatial patterns within Anglo-American house forms, suggesting that while spatial preference might transcend changes in house form, similar house plans might also contain different patterns of spatial use.[13] Therefore, form is not always a reliable indicator of a continuity or lack of continuity of spatial patterns.

In understanding the independence of social use and architectural form, we need not accept that they are totally unrelated. As we have seen, continuities in one facilitated changes in the other in southwestern North Carolina. Form and use often do appear, however, to constitute separate systems or structures. The grammar of architectural form may indeed provide a link to "past mind," but it does not tell us fully about architectural use, anymore than a linguistic grammar would tell about how people of a past culture spoke.[14] As the ethnography of speaking approach argues, generative grammar does not fully account for human communication because it does not consider the rules that govern social and cultural use of language. Architecture, like language, is organized around a "plurality of functions," and individual functions as well as structure warrant study.[15] Meaning is inherent in the rules that shape use as well as structure.

The evidence provided in this study suggests three limitations in interpreting social and symbolic use from physical form alone. The first is simply that the broad outlines of physical form do not fully articulate the complexities of use; we cannot understand the organization of the single pen house from its simple form. Second is the suggestion that house plan and spatial use are to some degree independent. As we have seen in chapter 3, different forms may accommodate a single system of spatial use or a single form may accommodate more than one system of spatial organization. Finally, chapters 4 and 5 suggest the problems posed by the multiplicity of functions of the dwelling to artifactual analysis. The center-passage I-house was adopted by some, perhaps for its symbolic implications, but users often refused to accommodate their system of spatial use to it. Therefore the form is a misleading artifact of spatial use. As seen in chapter 5, changing functions may also affect the physical preservation of the structure.

For those interested in the preservation of rural structures, chapter 5 is suggestive. Often when buildings are abandoned or destroyed we presume that people do not know the meaning of their own structures and that this problem can be rectified by educational programs. However, the destruction and abandonment of old houses does not necessarily result from a lack of meaning ascribed to them. In southwestern North Carolina the strength of the symbolic role of the homeplace is actually an agent of the "abuse" of old houses. The rural people of southwestern North Carolina realize that the old house is a symbol. Unlike some preservationists and vernacular architecture scholars, they do not place their value on the physical nature of the house. A house does not have to be maintained to serve as a symbol, and in the absence of the house, an empty site or a well-preserved narrative will do. While these attitudes may have negative ramifications for those of us who study houses as artifacts of the past or aesthetically appreciate old buildings, can one argue that these people do not know the meaning of their old houses? Rather than educate the rural people of southwestern North Carolina to the meaning of old houses, we should take the time to allow them to educate us to the fact that meaning is not found in the tangible form alone.[16]

This study may also have implications for understanding certain types of documentary evidence, such as room nomenclature. While a name for a room may indeed demonstrate that it fits into a conceptual order, the lack of names does not necessarily indicate a lack of order.[17] Certainly, within some circumstances a lack of specific names may indicate a lack of social meaning, or a pattern of generalized room use, but this is not invariably the case.[18] In southwestern North Carolina, room nomenclature is, at best, vague, and there is an almost complete lack of typology of form. While this may be baffling to the interviewer, order itself is not lacking. People built a limited number of house types and obviously recognized the difference between them. The rooms within the house were defined in terms of meaning and function, although at times the meanings were complex and the uses, multilayered. While in terms of nomenclature, it might be "just a room," the individual always knew which room he or she was in, and what it was used for.

The evidence from southwestern North Carolina is also helpful in forming a better understanding of potential conflicts between the evidence of room nomenclature and that of actual room use as indicated, for instance, by inventories of possessions and furnishings. In this region the central passage usually continued to be called a hall although its actual use was often in conflict with the implied function. The parlor was defined conceptually in formal terms, in keeping with its name, although in actual use it was frequently used more often for the practical and private function of sleeping family members. Lacking oral testimony, weight should neither be given wholly to the evidence of nomenclature nor to actual use. Instead, the conflicting evidence might be interpreted as potentially being the product of functional conflict between an idealized social milieu and actual social behavior.

Oral testimony is certainly not the only means by which we can understand architectural use and meaning. More than providing evidence for a certain period of time, however, it does allow us to explore the limitations of understanding various phenomena through different types of evidence, and it may suggest alternative possibilities for the interpretation of data. This is not to suggest that studies based on oral testimony should become mere fodder for ethnographic analogy. While the study of architectural use in southwestern North Carolina through oral history may aid the understanding of folk architecture of a more distant past, particularly of culturally and historically related architectural forms, the evidence is only suggestive. There are no broad cross-cultural rules for understanding architectural use and meaning. Our conclusions need to be well-grounded in a limited historical and cultural context.

Folk architecture studies have differed from other folkloristic material culture studies in that they have treated their subject primarily as an artifact. The implication of this difference is not just that folk architecture scholars are more interested in the material culture of the past than the present, but that our actual subject of study *is* the past. While the search for deeper meanings is commendable in folk architecture research, the emphasis on artifactual analysis risks the limitations of viewing architecture only as evidence, rather than as an inherently interesting cultural phenomenon.[19]

Architecture is infinitely complex. As Gaston Bachelard argues in *The Poetics of Space*, it is difficult to go beyond the physical nature of the house as "a house is first and foremost a geometrical object, one which we are tempted to analyze rationally. Its prime reality is visible and tangible, made of well hewn solids and well fitted framework."[20] However, the structure is not just a tangible object, it is an ordering of empty space. Not only are the meanings and uses of architecture intangible, but, too, the essential social phenomenon of architecture is the ordered space rather than the object.[21] All items of material culture have intangible aspects of use and meaning, but few have the power to physically order human perception and behavior while at the same time serving as a visual symbol and a functional object. Of course, students of culture do not wish to study architecture solely for its own sake; but, prior to reducing it to the status of artifact, we need to understand the nature of architecture and how it differs from other tangible, cultural objects. Rather than always employing the study of architecture to understand human thought and behavior, we need also to employ our means of studying human thought and behavior in order to understand architecture.

NOTES

Introduction. Reinhabiting the House Through Narrative

1. For the purpose of this study, southwestern North Carolina consists of these eleven counties: Buncombe, Cherokee, Clay, Graham, Haywood, Henderson, Jackson, Macon, Madison, Swain, and Transylvania. Although all regional boundaries are to some extent arbitrary, this area has a high degree of cultural, historical, and geographical integrity.

2. When I began my work in North Carolina, the eleven-county area had all been surveyed at least once. Beginning in 1979, Douglas Swaim carried out a comprehensive survey of Buncombe County and Margaret Counts Owen conducted a reconnaissance survey of the other ten counties. From June 1980 to January 1981, I surveyed Henderson County and from June 1981 to January 1982, I conducted a survey of Cherokee County. Randall Cotton surveyed Haywood County in 1982 and 1983. Publications based on these surveys are: Douglas Swaim, *Cabins and Castles: The History and Architecture of Buncombe County, North Carolina* (Asheville: Historic Resources Commission of Asheville and Buncombe County, 1981), and Michael Ann Williams, *Marble and Log: The History and Architecture of Cherokee County, North Carolina* (Murphy, N.C.: Cherokee County Historical Museum Council, 1984). Unpublished reports and project files are located at the North Carolina Division of Archives and History, Western Office, Asheville, North Carolina.

3. See Mihaly Csikszentmihalyi and Eugene Rochberg-Halton, *The Meaning of Things: Domestic Symbols and Self* (Cambridge: Cambridge University Press, 1981), p. 124.

4. Charles E. Martin, *Hollybush: Folk Building and Social Change in an Appalachian Community* (Knoxville: University of Tennessee Press, 1984), pp. 15–16.

5. Tape recorded interview with Frances Bryson, Cowee community, Macon County, N.C., 26 July 1984.

6. Tape recorded interview with Katherine Porter, Rose Creek community, Macon County, N.C., 3 August 1984.

7. Tape recorded interview with Frank Messer, West Waynesville, Haywood County, N.C., 6 September 1984.

8. Tape recorded interview with Lolita Dean, Burningtown community, Macon County, N.C., 10 August 1984.

9. Interview with George Woodard, Bryson City, Swain County, N.C., 7 August 1984.

10. George W. McDaniel in *Hearth and Home: Preserving a People's Culture* (Philadelphia: Temple University Press, 1982), p. 85, cites a similar account from a black Marylander who was born in 1878. James Scriber's assertion that "you didn't get cold" and "everyone, you know, had the same pill to take" is almost identical in attitude to the accounts collected from western North Carolinians.

11. Gaston Bachelard, in *The Poetics of Space*, trans. Maria Jolas (Boston: Beacon Press, 1969), p. 40, develops the idea of the winter landscape as a simplified cosmos, sharpening the dialectic between house and universe. The winter landscape represents "non-house."

12. Tape recorded interview with Grady Carringer, Stecoah community, Graham County, N.C., 14 September 1984.

Chapter One. People and Place

1. For accounts of Cherokee prehistory, see Bennie C. Keel, *Cherokee Archaeology: A Study of the Appalachian Summit* (Knoxville: University of Tennessee Press, 1976), and Roy S. Dickens, Jr., *Cherokee Prehistory: The Pisgah Phase in the Appalachian Summit Region* (Knoxville: University of Tennessee Press, 1976).

2. See Keel, *Cherokee Archaeology*, p. 214–16, and Dickens, *Cherokee Prehistory*, pp. 14, 16–101.

3. William Bartram, *Travels Through North and South Carolina, Georgia, East and West Florida* (Facsimile of 1792 London Edition; Savannah, Ga.: Beehive Press, 1973), p. 365.

4. Quoted in Jerry Clyde Cashion, "Fort Butler and the Cherokee Indian Removal from North Carolina" (Draft report prepared for the North Carolina State Division of Archives and History, 1970), p. 2.

5. Tyler Blethen and Curtis Wood, Jr., *From Ulster to Carolina: The Migration of the Scotch-Irish to Southwestern North Carolina* (Cullowhee, N.C.: Western Carolina University, 1983).

6. Henry Glassie argues that the square cabin has English antecedents, while the rectangular cabin is of a northern Irish origin. He also suggests that the height of the story-and-a-half cabin shows a Pennsylvania German influence. See Henry Glassie, "The Types of the Southern Mountain Cabin," in *The Study of American Folklore*, ed. Jan Brunvand (New York: W. W. Norton & Co., 1968), pp. 338–70.

7. See Michael Southern, "The I-House as a Carrier of Style in Three Counties of the Northeastern Piedmont," in *Carolina Dwelling*, ed. Doug Swaim (Student Publication of the School of Design, Volume 26; Raleigh: North Carolina State University, 1978), pp. 70–83, for a discussion of the I-house in the North Carolina piedmont.

8. For a history of logging in this region, see Ronald D. Eller, *Miners, Millhands, and Mountaineers: Industrialization of the Appalachian South, 1880–1930* (Knoxville: University of Tennessee Press, 1982), pp. 86–127.

9. The state of Washington was one of the most popular destinations for western Carolinians seeking work. Many of the individuals interviewed for this study still have family in the Northwest.

10. A ground-breaking study of box construction in another part of Appalachia is Martin's *Hollybush*. His description of box construction in eastern Kentucky generally stands true for southwestern North Carolina, except that boxed houses in North Carolina were seldom heated with coal. I am indebted to Blanton Owen for initially bringing to my attention the existence of this type of construction in western North Carolina.

11. Tape recorded interview with Robert Blanton, Matlock Creek, Macon County, N.C., 3 July 1984.

12. Tape recorded interview with Jim Neal, Aquone community, Macon County, N.C., 2 August 1984.

13. Tape recorded interview with Bass Hyatt, Brasstown, Clay County, N.C., 21 September 1984.

14. Tape recorded interview with Jessie Frazier, Cullowhee, Jackson County, N.C., 21 July 1984.

15. One woman described living on a farm accessible only by farm sled while her male family members were fighting in World War II.

16. Of the individuals interviewed for this study, two are active ballad singers. Berzilla Wallin is from Sodom-Laurel, a community well known for its singers. Now in her nineties, Berzilla remembers Cecil Sharp visiting her community when she was a young woman, although she was not permitted to sing for the noted collector of traditional ballads. Kate Rogers also sings traditional ballads as well as sacred and popular songs. For a number of years, Kate sang these songs on her own radio show on a local station. Letha Hicks is the daughter of the noted ballad singer Margaret Packard. Several others, including Eller Garrett, remember their parents singing the old "love songs."

17. For a discussion of the continuity of folk building traditions (especially in the modern mobile home) along the Cumberland River in Tennessee and Kentucky, see Benita J. Howell, *A Survey of Folklife Along the Big South Fork of the Cumberland River* (Report of Investigations, No. 30, Dept. of Anthropology, University of Tennessee, Knoxville, 1981), p. 96.

Chapter Two. Big House: Use of the Single Pen Plan

1. Tape recorded interview with Kate Rogers, Ellijay community, Macon County, N.C., 3 October 1983.

2. Tape recorded interview with Addie Norton, Otto community, Macon County, N.C., 18 July 1984.

3. Tape recorded interview with Eller Garrett, Unaka community, Cherokee County, N.C., 20 June 1984.

4. Kate Rogers interview, 3 October 1983.

5. Tape recorded interview with Mary Jane Queen, John's Creek, Jackson County, N.C., 24 August 1984.

6. French Haynes (tape recorded interview, Clyde, Haywood County, N.C.,

25 July 1984) and Katherine Porter (tape recorded interview, Rose Creek, Macon County, N.C., 3 August 1984), both descendants of wealthy landowners, used the term in this manner.

7. This is particularly prevalent among those individuals who lived in both single pen and larger houses during their youth. Considering the high degree of rebuilding, as well as partitioning of and adding on to single pen houses during the early twentieth century, it is not surprising that there should be some broadening of the meaning of the term.

8. Hans Kurath, *A Word Geography of the Eastern United States* (Ann Arbor: University of Michigan Press, 1949), p. 51. The *Dictionary of American Regional English* notes that this use of the term "big house" is found chiefly in the South Midland region. Similar to Kurath, it defines "big house" as a living room, although one 1954 Tennessee reference defines it as the "room where members of the family spend most of their time together." Frederic G. Cassidy, *Dictionary of American Regional English*, Volume 1, *Introduction and A–C* (Cambridge: Harvard University Press, Belknap Press, 1985), pp. 233–34.

9. See John Demos, *A Little Commonwealth: Family Life in Plymouth Colony* (New York: Oxford University Press, 1970), pp. 24–51; Robert Blair St. George, "A Retreat from the Wilderness: Pattern in the Domestic Environments of Southeastern New England, 1630–1730" (Ph.D. dissertation, University of Pennsylvania, 1982); and M. W. Barley, *The English Farmhouse and Cottage* (London: Routledge and Kegan Paul, 1961).

10. Maurice Barley, "A Glossary of Names for Rooms in Houses of the Sixteenth and Seventeenth Centuries," in *Culture and Environment: Essays in Honour of Sir Cyril Fox*, ed. I. L. L. Foster and L. Alcock (London: Routledge and Kegan Paul, 1963), pp. 491–92; R. W. Brunskill, *Vernacular Architecture of the Lake Counties* (Boston: Faber and Faber, Faber Paperback Edition, 1978), p. 51; and St. George, "Retreat from the Wilderness," p. 365. *The English Dialect Dictionary* indicates that the term "house" to mean living room was still used in southwest England as late as 1893. Joseph Wright, *The English Dialect Dictionary* (Oxford: Henry Frowde, 1905).

11. Barley, *The English Farmhouse and Cottage*, p. 46.

12. Barley, "A Glossary of Names for Rooms," p. 488–89.

13. Thomas C. Hubka, "The Connected Farm Buildings of Southwestern Maine," *Pioneer America* 9 (1977): 143–78. Hubka refers to an old chil-

dren's rhyme that names the parts of the connected farmhouse as "big house, little house, back house, barn."

14. Tape recorded interview with Arvel Greene, Wilmont, Jackson County, N.C., 18 June 1984.

15. An example of this building pattern is the Walker family home on the Tennessee side of the Great Smoky Mountains National Park. In Robert R. Madden and T. Russell Jones, *Mountain Home—The Walker Family Homestead* (Washington, D.C.: U.S. Department of Interior, 1977), Madden uses the term "big house" in reference to the main block (upstairs and partitioned downstairs) of the dwelling.

16. *Oxford English Dictionary*, s.v. "big"; and *A Dictionary of the Older Scottish Tongue from the Twelfth Century to the End of the Seventeenth*, ed. Sir William A. Craigie (Chicago: University of Chicago Press, 1937), s.v. "big." I am grateful to Jan Davidson for originally suggesting the connection between "big house" and the Scottish "biggin."

17. Tape recorded interview with Zena Bennett, Iotla community, Macon County, N.C., 18 October 1983.

18. Eller Garrett interview.

19. Tape recorded interview with Monroe Ledford, Union community, Macon County, N.C., 21 October 1983.

20. Tape recorded interview with Oma Jenkins, Stecoah, Graham County, N.C., 23 May 1984. The comment was interjected by Mrs. Jenkins's daughter, Hilda.

21. Tape recorded interview with Bass Hyatt, Brasstown, Clay County, N.C., 21 September 1984.

22. Tape recorded interview with Letha Hicks, Big Bend community, Haywood County, N.C., 8 September 1984.

23. Tape recorded interview with Mary Messer, West Waynesville, Haywood County, N.C., 6 September 1984.

24. Mary Jane Queen interview.

25. Zena Bennett interview.

26. Tape recorded interview with Robert Blanton, Matlock Creek, Macon County, N.C., 3 July 1984.

27. Robert Blanton interview; tape recorded interview with Mike Rogers, Anderson Branch, Graham County, N.C., 27 January 1984.

28. Mike Rogers interview.

29. Eller Garrett interview.

30. Addie Norton interview.
31. Kate Rogers interview, 3 October 1983.
32. Tape recorded interview with Essie Moore, Caney Fork, Jackson County, N.C., 5 September 1984.
33. Kate Rogers interview, 17 July 1984.
34. Tape recorded interview with Lolita Dean, Burningtown community, Macon County, N.C., 10 August 1984.
35. Arvel Greene interview.
36. Kate Rogers interview, 3 October 1983.
37. Kate Rogers interview, 3 October 1983.
38. Letha Hicks interview.
39. Kate Rogers interview, 17 July 1984.
40. Kate Rogers interview, 3 October 1983.
41. Martin, *Hollybush*, pp. 83–84, 94–95.
42. Arvel Greene interview.
43. Monroe Ledford interview.
44. Csikszentmihalyi and Rochberg-Halton in *The Meaning of Things*, pp. 123–24, note that in El Salvador where 60 percent of all families live in one-room units, people rarely complain of feeling crowded.
45. Arvel Greene interview.
46. Tape recorded interview with Grady Carringer, Stecoah, Graham County, N.C., 14 September 1984.
47. Essie Moore interview.
48. Robert Blanton interview.
49. Zena Bennett interview.
50. Tape recorded interview with Willa Mae Pressley, Bo Cove, Jackson County, N.C., 28 June 1984.
51. Monroe Ledford interview.
52. Tape recorded interview with Gilford Williams, Stecoah, Graham County, N.C., 4 October 1983.
53. Zena Bennett interview.
54. Tape recorded interview with Anna Collett, Valleytown, Cherokee County, N.C., 13 October 1983.
55. Witold Rybczynski suggests that the concept of domestic privacy does not develop unless people no longer live and work in the same place. In his study of privacy in colonial New England, David Flaherty suggests that the intimacy of the family encompassed the rural community. See Witold Rybczyn-

ski, *Home: A Short History of an Idea* (New York: Viking, 1986), p. 39; and David H. Flaherty, *Privacy in Colonial New England* (Charlottesville: University Press of Virginia, 1972), p. 2. For an ethnographic study of the achievement of personal privacy in courting behavior despite the lack of private interior space, see Gerald Lewis Pocius, "Privacy and Architecture: A Newfoundland Example," paper presented to the annual meeting of the Vernacular Architecture Forum, Salt Lake City, Utah, May 1987.

56. Tape recorded interview with Bessie Tilley, Tilley Creek, Jackson County, N.C., 9 July 1984.

57. Flaherty suggests that facets of the concept of privacy include solitude, intimacy, anonymity, reserve, and that "mutual understanding, long friendships, and kinship are normally as protective and restorative for the individual as solitude." *Privacy in Colonial New England*, p. 2.

58. See discussion of the parlor in the following chapter.

59. Eller Garrett interview.

60. Addie Norton interview.

61. Arvel Greene interview.

62. Monroe Ledford interview.

63. Letha Hicks interview.

64. Mary Jane Queen interview.

65. The partitioned single room plan is also found in England and early New England. See R. W. Brunskill, *Illustrated Handbook of Vernacular Architecture*, 2d ed. (Boston: Faber and Faber, 1978), pp. 104–5; and Demos, *A Little Commonwealth*, pp. 30–31.

66. Kate Rogers interviews, Monroe Ledford interview.

67. Letha Hicks interview.

68. Tape recorded interview with Larry Gunter, Ninevah community, Haywood County, N.C., 31 August 1984.

69. Arvel Greene interview.

70. Tape recorded interview with Fanny Fisher, Addie community, Jackson County, N.C., 28 August 1984.

71. Martin, *Hollybush*, p. 79, notes that people would rather double up than sleep where food was prepared in the Hollybush community in eastern Kentucky. This was true in western North Carolina only when the kitchen was in a functionally separate room. As we have seen, some people continued to eat and sleep in one room, suggesting that it has more to do with

the nature of how the room is conceptualized rather than an aversion to combining the functions.

72. Fanny Fisher used this phrase to describe this arrangement.

73. Robert Blanton interview, Arvel Greene interview.

74. Tape recorded interview with Tiny Arms, Owl Creek, Cherokee County, N.C., 10 July 1984.

75. Bessie Tilley interview.

76. Tape recorded interview with Berzilla Wallin, Sodom-Laurel, Madison County, N.C., 28 July 1984.

77. Parlors were traditionally found in the double pen house, but not in the partitioned single pen house. In terms of spatial use, the double pen plan is more akin to the hall and parlor houses found elsewhere in the eastern United States.

78. Willa Mae Pressley, one of the younger informants, was the only one who reported that in her family the children slept near the hearth, while the parents slept in another room.

79. Tape recorded interview with Minnie McDonald, Hanging Dog community, Cherokee County, N.C., 27 August 1984.

80. R. O. Wilson, who was born in the 1930s, reported a fairly traditional pattern of spatial use within his family. His homeplace was a single pen, framed, board and batten house with a living room (where the parents slept), a back room, and a rear shed kitchen. Tape recorded interview with R. O. Wilson, Wilson Creek, Jackson County, N.C., 5 October 1983.

81. Tape recorded interview with Vestal Cochran, Nantahala, Macon County, N.C., 26 June 1984.

82. This comment was prompted by the fact that Mrs. Frazier's daughter, who was present at the interview, expressed surprise that she had never heard the term "big house," after her mother talked about its meaning. Tape recorded interview with Jessie Frazier, Cullowhee, Jackson County, N.C., 21 July 1984.

83. Zena Bennett interview.

84. Kate Rogers interview, 3 October 1983.

85. Oma Jenkins interview.

86. Martin, in *Hollybush*, pp. 82–83, notes the cooperative building of "offspring houses," very small single pen houses for newly married couples in the eastern Kentucky community he studied. I did not find any strong

evidence for this pattern in southwestern North Carolina that can be clearly separated from the changing economic conditions and the growing preference for more rooms. Some people built very small homes due to the need to follow available work. As we have seen, some people raised large families in small houses that were never substantially expanded. The more intensive study of individual communities within this region, however, might reveal building patterns similar to those found in Hollybush.

87. Addie Norton interview.

Chapter Three. *Rethinking the House: The Double Pen Plan*

1. The term "dogtrot" is sometimes used, but usually it is in reference to a connecting walkway between the house and the kitchen, rather than a true dogtrot plan. Furthermore its current use seems heavily influenced by local color writers; the older term is probably "passageway." Eller Garrett also used the term "pen" humorously to describe small one-room houses. Tape recorded interview with Eller Garrett, Unaka community, Cherokee County, N.C., 20 June 1984.

2. Tape recorded interview with Arvel Greene, Wilmont, Jackson County, N.C., 18 June 1984; tape recorded interview with Kate Rogers, Ellijay community, Macon County, N.C., 3 October 1983; and tape recorded interview with Monroe Ledford, Union community, Macon County, N.C., 21 October 1983.

3. Tape recorded interview with R. O. Wilson, Wilson Creek, Jackson County, N.C., 5 October 1983.

4. Eller Garrett interview.

5. Tape recorded interview with Nanny Potts Sorrells, Cowee community, Macon County, N.C., 12 October 1983.

6. Tape recorded interview with Fanny Fisher, Addie community, Jackson County, N.C., 28 August 1984.

7. Fanny Fisher interview.

8. Tape recorded interview with Jessie Frazier, Cullowhee, Jackson County, N.C., 21 July 1984. Thomas Hubka notes that the term "double house" was widely used in eighteenth- and nineteenth-century New England to describe the center chimney hall and parlor house, indicating that one-room houses were probably still common and that these houses were perceived

as two whole units. Thomas C. Hubka, *Big House, Little House, Back House, Barn: The Connected Farm Buildings of New England* (Hanover: University Press of New England, 1984), pp. 47–48.

9. Eugene M. Wilson, *Alabama Folk Houses* (Montgomery: Alabama Historical Commission, 1975), pp. 25, 45; and Allen G. Noble, *Wood, Brick, and Stone: The North American Settlement Landscape*, vol. 1, *Houses* (Amherst: University of Massachusetts Press, 1984), pp. 115–17. Terry Jordan, in *American Log Buildings: An Old World Heritage* (Chapel Hill: University of North Carolina Press, 1985), finds various Scandinavian and British antecedents to the double pen plans. See also Martin Wright, "The Antecedents of the Double Pen House Type," *Annals of the Association of American Geographers* 48, no. 2 (1958): 109–17.

10. Other names for the English hall were "fireroom," "firehouse," and "house." Barley, "A Glossary of Names for Rooms," pp. 488–92.

11. The "other room" of the partitioned single pen plan does resemble the "inner room" of the small English house that functionally developed into the parlor by the sixteenth century, but it does not have the formal purposes associated with later American and English hall and parlor houses despite the fact that its proportions perhaps more closely resemble the hall and parlor plan than does the symmetrical double pen plan. Demos, *A Little Commonwealth*, p. 46; and Barley, "A Glossary of Names for Rooms," pp. 496–97.

12. Monroe Ledford interview.

13. Fanny Fisher interview.

14. Tape recorded interview with Vestal Cochran, Nantahala community, Macon County, N.C., 26 June 1984.

15. Barley, "A Glossary of Names for Rooms," pp. 496–97. In his study of a community in Northern Ireland, Henry Glassie speaks of the "ancient duality of the parlor, a place for nighttime sleeping and daytime withdrawing." Glassie, *Passing the Time in Ballymenone: Culture and History of an Ulster Community* (Philadelphia: University of Pennsylvania Press, 1982), p. 381.

16. Carl Lounsbury, "The Development of Domestic Architecture in the Albemarle Region," in *Carolina Dwelling*, ed. Doug Swaim, Student Publication of the School of Design, vol. 26 (Raleigh: North Carolina State University, 1978), p. 50. Abbott Lowell Cummings, *The Framed Houses of Massachusetts Bay, 1625–1725* (Cambridge: Harvard University Press, Belknap

Press, 1979), p. 28; and St. George, "A Retreat from the Wilderness," pp. 344–47. In New England, the parlor as "best sleeping chamber" was usually the parents' bedroom, while in southwestern North Carolina the parlor was a guest bedroom or was used to sleep children.

17. Interview with Jonathan Woody, conducted by George Richardson and Sam Easterby, Waynesville, Haywood County, N.C., 27 February 1973. Transcript located in N.C. Collection, Haywood County Public Library, Waynesville, North Carolina.

18. Monroe Ledford interview.

19. Erving Goffman's observations on region behavior are useful in understanding the parlor. The room, a "front region," may revert in actual use to a "back region" when a "performance" (formal interaction) is not taking place. *The Presentation of Self in Everyday Life* (Garden City, N.Y.: Doubleday, Anchor Books, 1959), pp. 156–57.

20. For instance, Hubka in *Big House, Little House, Back House, Barn*, p. 36, notes that the parlor in New England was used most of the time as a combination bedroom and storage room rather than as a place for formal interaction. The evidence of actual use, however, does not necessarily mean that the room did not fill a formal role symbolically, if not socially.

21. Thomas Adler's study of folk housing in the Blue Ridge of southern Virginia and northern North Carolina also notes that informants reported a reluctance to fully utilize the upstairs, indicating that the sharing of sleeping and working areas is not necessarily a result of limited space. Adler suggests that this attitude was part of a move *toward* single story dwellings, although the evidence for southwestern North Carolina indicates that the attitude was deeply rooted in tradition. Thomas A. Adler, "Toward an Ecology of Folk Housing in the East-Central Blue Ridge," unpublished manuscript.

22. Tape recorded interview with Anna Collett, Valleytown, Cherokee County, N.C., 13 October 1983.

23. In post-medieval England most people continued to cook in the hall. The kitchen, when present, was detached (a tradition stemming from the Middle Ages) and was not considered part of the house. This duality of either preparing food in the social center of the house or of relegating it to an outbuilding was continued throughout the nineteenth century in rural southwestern North Carolina. See Barley, *The English Farmhouse and Cottage*, pp. 63, 76.

24. See Glassie, *Passing the Time in Ballymenone*, pp. 381–98, for an interpretation of the separation of the kitchen from the social center of the house in Northern Ireland.

25. A movement toward an equality of room size also occurred in the central chimney hall and parlor house in New England during the eighteenth century.

26. Other studies have also noted instances of patterns of domestic spatial use transcending changes in house form. See Gerald Lewis Pocius, "Calvert: A Study of Artifacts and Spatial Usage in a Newfoundland Community" (Ph.D. dissertation, University of Pennsylvania, 1979), p. 292; and Susan Kent, *Analyzing Activity Areas: An Ethnoarchaeological Study of the Use of Space* (Albuquerque: University of New Mexico Press, 1984), pp. 133–34. Kent observes that the use of space by Navajos who live in modern multi-room rectangular houses is more similar to that of other Navajos living in circular hogans than it is to Euroamericans living in identical modern houses.

27. For instance, in *Hearth and Home*, pp. 26–28, 214–17, George W. McDaniel reports oral testimony of a conservative "hall and parlor" spatial organization (a room that was the center of family life and a parlor that was also used as a bedroom) maintained well into the twentieth century. McDaniel's observation on the organization of space within a single room house also shows striking similarities to the spatial organization in southwestern North Carolina.

28. Monroe Ledford interview.

29. Anna Collett interview.

30. Vestal Cochran interview.

31. Tape recorded interview with Essie Moore, Caney Fork, Jackson County, N.C., 5 September 1984.

32. Essie Moore interview.

33. Tape recorded interview with Lolita Dean, Burningtown community, Macon County, N.C., 10 August 1984.

34. Anna Collett interview.

35. Tape recorded interview with Leo Gibson, Cowee community, Macon County, N.C., 12 October 1983.

36. Tape recorded interview with Eula Sheffield Bryson, Cowee community, Macon County, N.C., 12 October 1983.

37. Monroe Ledford interview.

38. On alteration of houses, see Elizabeth Collins Cromley, "Modernization; Or, 'You Never See a Screen Door on Affluent Homes,'" *Journal of American Culture* 5, no. 2 (Summer 1982): 71–79; Yvonne J. Milspaw, "Reshaping Tradition: Changes to Pennsylvania German Folk Houses," *Pioneer America: The Journal of Historic Material Culture* 15, no. 2 (July 1983): 67–84; Michael Owen Jones, "L.A. Add-ons and Re-dos: Renovation in Folk Art and Architectural Design," in *Perspectives on American Folk Art*, ed. Ian M. G. Quimby and Scott T. Swank (New York: W. W. Norton, 1980), pp. 325–63; and Pocius, "Calvert," pp. 374–75. Also see articles by Gerald L. Pocius, Bernard L. Herman, Michael Ann Williams, Thomas Carter, and Elizabeth Mosby Adler in the special issue on remodeling in *Material Culture* 19, nos. 2–3 (1987).

39. In earlier fieldwork conducted during the summer of 1978 in the Tennessee Hills of northeast Mississippi, I collected oral testimony of similar spatial changes without physical alteration of double pen plan houses. This included testimony about dogtrot plans and double pen plans with exterior end chimneys, indicating that these changes took place in all variations of the "double pen" houses, and this pattern was not restricted only to southwestern North Carolina. Michael Ann Williams, "The Use of Vernacular Architecture in the Rural South: Some Observations and Directions for Further Research," unpublished manuscript.

40. Unlike in some parts of the South where the southern bungalow with its front facing gable was rapidly accepted, the shotgun plan is generally not found in rural southwestern North Carolina. Therefore the bungalow was the first plan to introduce the reorientation of the gable to the rural countryside in this region.

41. After describing several log and plank houses of his childhood, Gilford Williams mentioned that he thought Mike Rogers's house, a small bungalow with a front facing gable built during the 1930s, was an "old-time house." Tape recorded interview with Gilford Williams, Stecoah community, Graham County, N.C., 4 October 1983.

42. Anna Collett interview.

Chapter Four. The Center Passage: Conflict in Function

1. The widespread distribution of the "I-house" has been noted since the 1930s when cultural geographer Fred Kniffen named the plan after the Illinois, Iowa, and Indiana origins of its prairie Louisiana builders (as well as the house's profile). In Kniffen's description, the I-house is characterized by "gables to the side, at least two rooms in length, one room deep, and two full stories in height." In more recent scholarship, however, the term I-house is frequently associated with its most common variant, the center-passage plan. Although the term is problematic, no accurate and concise substitute has received widespread acceptance. See Fred Kniffen, "Folk Housing: Key to Diffusion," *Annals of the Association of American Geographers* 55 (December 1955): 553.

2. See Henry Glassie, *Folk Housing in Middle Virginia: A Structural Analysis of Historic Artifacts* (Knoxville: University of Tennessee Press, 1975), pp. 120–21, 182–93; and his "Eighteenth-Century Cultural Process in Delaware Valley Folk Building," *Winterthur Portfolio* 7 (1972): 44–45. For other interpretations of center passages and hallways as social locks see Dell Upton, "Vernacular Domestic Architecture in Eighteenth Century Virginia," *Winterthur Portfolio* 17 (Summer/Autumn 1982): 103–4; St. George, "A Retreat from the Wilderness," p. 162; Lounsbury, "The Development of Domestic Architecture in the Albemarle Region," p. 51; and Simon Bronner, "Manner Books and Suburban Houses: The Structure of Traditional Aesthetics," *Winterthur Portfolio* 18 (1983): 65.

3. It may be argued that the I-house's center passage originally represented a coincidence of environmental, social, and symbolic functions. However, it should be noted that the spatial use of the hallway in a way which draws full benefit from the cooling effects may be quite different from the use of the passage as a social lock. Architectural historian Mark Wenger effectively argues that while the eighteenth-century Virginia planter elite may have initially accepted the center passage as an instrument of social control, they soon discovered its environmental benefits, ultimately converting the formal passage into a socially prestigious living space. Mark R. Wenger, "The Central Passage in Virginia: Evolution of an Eighteenth-Century Living Space," in *Perspectives in Vernacular Architecture, II*, ed. Camille Wells (Columbia: University of Missouri Press, 1986), pp. 137–49.

See also Michael Southern, "The I-House as a Carrier of Style in Three Counties of the Northeastern Piedmont," p. 82.

4. John C. Inscoe, "Mountain Masters: Slaveholding in Western North Carolina," *North Carolina Historical Review* 60 (1983): 171. Between 1840 and 1860, the increase in slave population in the mountain counties was greater than in the rest of the state.

5. See Williams, *Marble and Log*, pp. 29–31, and "The Architecture of Henderson County, North Carolina," unpublished report, on file at North Carolina Division of Archives and History, Western Office, Asheville, N.C.

6. Of the major slave owners in Cherokee County in 1860, Joshua Harshaw owned 33 slaves; A. H. Sudderth, 30; R. D. McCombs (agent for John Sudderth), 19; Abram Harshaw heirs, 43; and Abraham Sudderth, 26. The majority of rural slaveholders owned considerably fewer. Not all slaveholders in the region were rural, however. Inscoe, "Mountain Masters," argues that a large number of slaves in western North Carolina were used for non-agricultural purposes.

7. Interview with Polly Stewart McGuire, Andrews, Cherokee County, N.C., 25 August 1981; tape recorded interview with Eller Garrett, Unaka community, Cherokee County, N.C., 20 June 1984.

8. Williams, *Marble and Log*, pp. 29–31, 40, 114.

9. Tape recorded interview with Bass Hyatt, Brasstown, Clay County, N.C., 21 September 1984; tape recorded interview with Lolita Dean, Burningtown, Macon County, N.C., 10 August 1984; and tape recorded interview with Oma Jenkins, Stecoah, Graham County, N.C., 23 May 1984. Bass Hyatt moved from a center-passage house to a single pen house and back to a center-passage house when he was a child; Lolita Dean's mother was raised in a center-passage house but lived in a saddlebag house after she married; Oma Jenkins was born in a single pen house, raised in a double pen house, and lived in a center-passage house after she was married.

10. Lounsbury, "The Development of Domestic Architecture in the Albemarle Region," p. 51.

11. Interview with Maudine Martin, Bell View community, Cherokee County, N.C., 22 June 1981.

12. Thomas Carter found that mid-twentieth-century occupants of nineteenth-century center-passage houses in central Utah often chose to remove the central passage. The later occupants found the hallway impractical and

"in the way." Thomas Carter, " 'It Was in the Way, So We Took It Out': Remodeling as Social Commentary," *Material Culture* 19 (1987): 113–25. For a study of recent alterations and alternative uses (including butchering a hog) in Pennsylvania German central-passage houses, see Charles Bergengren, "The Cycle of Transformations in Schaefferstown, Pennsylvania, Houses," paper presented to the annual meeting of the Vernacular Architecture Forum, May 1988.

13. The Julius McCoy House, which was destroyed by fire, was described by Lolita Dean, the builder's granddaughter. The two surviving houses in Cowee are the circa 1850 Hall House and the circa 1863 James Bryson House.

14. Tape recorded interview with French Haynes, Clyde, Haywood County, N.C., 25 July 1984.

15. Examples are the George Hayes House in Tomatla, Cherokee County, and the John W. Wells House in Sandy Mush, Buncombe County. Both were built during the mid-nineteenth century.

16. An example of an enclosed dogtrot with three front doors is the circa 1835 Thomas Tatham House near Andrews, believed to be the oldest surviving house in Cherokee County.

17. Lolita Dean interview.

18. Tape recorded interview with Katherine Porter, Rose Creek, Macon County, N.C., 3 August 1984.

19. Lolita Dean interview, Katherine Porter interview.

20. French Haynes interview.

21. Swaim, *Cabins and Castles*, pp. 66–67.

22. Interview with R. Stirewalt, Ranger community, Cherokee County, N.C., 2 November 1981.

23. Margaret Walker Freel, *Our Heritage: The People of Cherokee County, North Carolina* (Asheville, N.C.: Miller Printing Company, 1956), pp. 119–20.

24. Polly Stewart McGuire interview.

25. Haywood County files, North Carolina Division of Archives and History, Western Office, Asheville, N.C.

26. Bass Hyatt interview. Mr. Hyatt's wife, Lucy Moore Hyatt, remembers her grandfather's home, a two-story, mid-nineteenth-century central-passage house, as also having a parlor that had beds for company. Tape recorded

interview with Lucy Moore Hyatt, Brasstown, Clay County, N.C., 21 September 1984. The circa 1860 Captain Bill P. Moore House is still standing in the Tusquitee section of Clay County.

27. French Haynes interview.

28. Tape recorded interview with Frances Bryson, Cowee community, Macon County, N.C., 26 July 1984.

29. Oma Jenkins interview. Despite the fact that the hallway was used as a living area, it is interesting to note that in Mrs. Jenkins's description, as in the testimony of several other individuals, the hallway is still identified as a hall. The term is not used, however, in the older sense of the word as the main living space for it is never interchanged with the terms for living room. The concept of the space as a central passage seemed clear despite the fact that the hallway was actually used for a different purpose.

30. Susan Kent notes a similar situation in *Analyzing Activity Areas*, p. 197. Spanish-Americans and Navajos living in modern multi-room houses do not tend to utilize all the bedrooms available in their sleeping arrangements.

31. Tape recorded interview with Pearl Caldwell, Maggie Valley, Haywood County, N.C., 24 July 1984. The Hiram Caldwell House was built for Pearl Caldwell's father-in-law; the other house was built for her sister-in-law. Both were apparently built by the same carpenters. The house in Maggie Valley was located near a lumber camp.

32. Tape recorded interview with Nora Moody, Iotla community, Macon County, N.C., 24 September 1984.

33. J. Randall Cotton, "The Built Environment of Haywood County," report on file at North Carolina Division of Archives and History, Western Office, Asheville, N.C., pp. 5, 21, 22. Cotton notes that Cataloochee was a popular overnight destination for Waynesville-based tourists.

34. Pearl Caldwell interview.

35. Jackson County files, North Carolina Division of Archives and History, Western Office, Asheville, N.C.

36. Tape recorded interview with Vestal Cochran, Nantahala community, Macon County, N.C., 26 June 1984.

37. Mary Douglas, "Symbolic Orders in the Use of Domestic Space," in *Man, Settlement, and Urbanism*, ed. Peter J. Ucko, Ruth Tringham, and G. W. Dimbleby (London: Duckworth, 1972), pp. 514, 521.

38. See Anne Louise Gjesdal Christensen, "Dwellings as Communication,"

Ethnologia Scandinavica 9 (1979): 74, for distinctions between inward and outward communication.

39. Charles Joyner, *Down by the Riverside: A South Carolina Slave Community* (Urbana and Chicago: University of Illinois Press, 1984), pp. 117–26.

Chapter Five. Abandonment and the "Old Homeplace"

1. Tape recorded interview with Willa Mae Pressley, Bo Cove community, Jackson County, N.C., 28 June 1984.
2. A somewhat similar case is discussed in Pocius, "Calvert," pp. 375–81. Tradition is maintained through oral and interactional means, but there is little value placed on material aspects of tradition.
3. A large number of western North Carolinians followed the timber industry to the state of Washington. As Essie Moore reported, "All my brothers are in the state of Washington, where there's work. They all left to work." Or Jessie Frazier, "My brothers, as soon as they got old enough, they took off and went to the west." Tape recorded interview with Essie Moore, Caney Fork community, Jackson County, N.C., 5 September 1984; and tape recorded interview with Jessie Frazier, Cullowhee, Jackson County, N.C., 21 July 1984.
4. As well-intentioned as the creation of the Tennessee Valley Authority and the Great Smoky Mountains National Park may have been, the removal of families left a legacy of bitterness among many rural people in southwestern North Carolina. The creation of the park alone entailed the relocation of approximately one thousand families in North Carolina and Tennessee. The park removals demonstrate the powerlessness of those people who knew the area as home against the interests of a relatively urban, well-to-do group of park supporters who viewed the area as "wilderness." For a study of similar circumstances, see Charles L. Perdue, Jr., and Nancy J. Martin-Perdue, "Appalachian Fables and Facts: A Case Study of the Shenandoah National Park Removals," *Appalachian Journal* 7 (Autumn-Winter 1979–80): 84–104.
5. On most federally owned land (which in a few of the westernmost counties constitutes from a third to well over a half of the total area), architectural remnants of earlier owners have completely disappeared. This is particu-

larly true of the land that is part of the TVA and the National Forest, although much of the latter was created from denuded timber lands that had already been stripped of their signs of permanent occupance. Some structures were chosen to be left intact after the creation of the Great Smoky Mountains National Park. The selection process paralleled other regional processes of preservation by favoring the most and the least traditional structures, rather than those that represented the norm.

6. For a preservationist's analysis of the problems of rural abandonment in North Carolina, see Kathleen Pepi Southern, *Historic Preservation in Rural North Carolina: Problems and Potentials* (Raleigh: Historic Preservation Society of North Carolina, 1982), pp. 24–25.

7. Tape recorded interview with Arvel Greene, Wilmont, Jackson County, N.C., 18 June 1984.

8. In contrast, Glassie, in *Passing the Time in Ballymenone*, p. 344, reports that in Ballymenone, "home place" consists of the present homestead, including the outbuildings and surrounding yard.

9. Willa Mae Pressley interview.

10. Tape recorded interview with Oma Jenkins, Stecoah community, Graham County, N.C., 23 May 1984.

11. In this way the rural people of southwestern North Carolina differ from the people of Newfoundland, as documented by Pocius in "Calvert," p. 375. In Calvert, rebuilding was partially in response to a concern for being stylistically up-to-date, but in southwestern North Carolina, rural people rebuilt with relatively little concern for stylistic change. The pattern of rebuilding among every generation was apparently quite common among medieval peasants in England. See J. G. Hurst, "The Changing Medieval Village in England," in *Man, Settlement, and Urbanism*, ed. Peter J. Ucko, Ruth Tringham, and G. W. Dimbleby (London: Duckworth, 1972), p. 533.

12. Interview with Ernest Justus, Upward community, Henderson County, N.C., 13 August 1980.

13. Relatively few studies of folk architecture have dealt with these types of major alterations and the evolution of individual farmsteads. An exception is Hubka, *Big House, Little House, Back House, Barn*, pp. 27, 86–112. Hubka demonstrates that the process of alteration of farmsteads must be examined in order to understand the development of the connected farm.

14. Tape recorded interview with Bass Hyatt, Brasstown, Clay County, N.C., 21 September 1984.

15. Tape recorded interview with Katherine Porter, Rose Creek community, Macon County, N.C., 3 August 1984; and tape recorded interview with Frances Bryson, Cowee community, Macon County, N.C., 26 July 1984.

16. Tape recorded interview with French Haynes, Clyde, Haywood County, N.C., 25 July 1984.

17. See Williams, *Marble and Log*, pp. 29–31.

18. Oma Jenkins interview; tape recorded interview with Minnie McDonald, Hanging Dog community, Cherokee County, N.C., 27 August 1984; tape recorded interview with Monroe Ledford, Union community, Macon County, N.C., 21 October 1983; and tape recorded interview with Mary Jane Queen, John's Creek community, Jackson County, N.C., 24 August 1984.

19. Tape recorded interview with R. O. Wilson, Wilson Creek, Jackson County, N.C., 5 October 1983.

20. Tape recorded interview with Robert Blanton, Matlock Creek, Macon County, N.C., 3 July 1984.

21. Cary Carson, Norman F. Barka, William M. Kelso, Gary Wheeler Stone, and Dell Upton, "Impermanent Architecture in the Southern American Colonies," *Winterthur Portfolio* 16 (1981): 135–96.

22. These were the words used by Nanny Sorrells to describe her childhood home, a large log saddlebag house built by her grandfather. The house was torn down in 1936. Tape recorded interview with Nanny Potts Sorrells, Cowee community, Macon County, N.C., 12 October 1983.

23. See Martin, *Hollybush*, pp. 26–28, for a description of the building techniques involved in the construction of the Appalachian box or plank house.

24. Martin, *Hollybush*, pp. 17, 25–26, distinguishes between "pole" houses, early provisional shelters, and the later round-log house. In southwestern North Carolina, the term "pole" is commonly used for any house built of unhewn logs. Martin notes that while some builders believed that a round-log house would last as long as a hewn one, this was definitely not the case. The round-log house became popular in Hollybush in the 1930s when standards of appropriate longevity had changed so that the shortened life expectancy was accepted.

25. The building of vertical plank houses is generally associated with the avail-ability of local sawmills and the abundance of timber. See, for instance, Cummings, *The Framed Houses of Massachusetts Bay*, pp. 89–91.

26. Tape recorded interview with Grady Carringer, Stecoah community, Graham County, N.C., 14 September 1984.

27. The process of building plank houses in western North Carolina resulted in structures of limited permanence, but vertical plank houses are not necessarily inherently impermanent. Some examples of eighteenth-century plank houses in New England, which were clapboarded or shingled on the exterior and plastered on the interior, survived for two centuries. For a description of New England plank houses see Walter R. Nelson, "Some Examples of Plank House Construction and Their Origin," *Pioneer America* 1 (July 1969): 18–29; and Cummings, *The Framed Houses of Massachusetts Bay*, pp. 89–92. For a brief overview of plank building in the United States see Dell Upton, "Traditional Timber Framing," in *Material Culture of the Wooden Age*, ed. Brooke Hindle (Tarrytown, N.Y.: Sleepy Hollow Press, 1981), pp. 45–48.

28. Jessie Frazier grew up near the Sunburst timber camp in Haywood County. Log houses had been common in the area, but as Mrs. Frazier explained, "After Sunburst, and the sawmill came in there, they had plenty of lumber to do things. Then people went to building little, just boxed houses, boxed-up out of lumber." Tape recorded interview with Jessie Frazier, Cullowhee, Jackson County, N.C., 21 July 1984.

29. Tape recorded interview with Jim Neal, Aquone community, Macon County, N.C., 2 August 1984.

30. Although as noted in the example of R. O. Wilson's grandfather, it was not uncommon for a man to build more than one house during his life.

31. Tape recorded interview with Lucy Moore Hyatt, Brasstown, Clay County, N.C., 21 September 1984.

32. Tape recorded interview with Zena Bennett, Iotla community, Macon County, N.C., 18 October 1983.

33. Tape recorded interview with Larry Gunter, Ninevah community, Haywood County, N.C., 31 August 1984.

34. For an analysis of land inheritance in other parts of Appalachia, see F. Carlene Bryant, *We're All Kin: A Cultural Study of a Mountain Neighborhood* (Knoxville: University of Tennessee Press, 1981), pp. 66–74; and Patricia Duane Beaver, *Rural Community in the Appalachian South* (Lexington: University Press of Kentucky, 1986), pp. 64–72. Beaver, in her study of three communities in northwest North Carolina, found that the ideal of equal inheritance was modified by several factors, including

preference for the youngest child, some preference for males (particularly if they were working the land), outmigration, and current land prices.

35. Tape recorded interview with Lolita Dean, Burningtown community, Macon County, N.C., 10 August 1984.

36. Nanny Potts Sorrells interview.

37. Minnie McDonald interview.

38. Tape recorded interview with Mary Messer, West Waynesville, Haywood County, N.C., 6 September 1984.

39. Jim Neal interview.

40. Tape recorded interview with Bessie Tilley, Tilley Creek, Jackson County, N.C., 9 July 1984.

41. Arvel Greene interview.

42. Oma Jenkins interview. Mrs. Jenkins's daughter, Hilda, was present at the interview.

43. Tape recorded interview with Anna Collett, Valleytown community, Cherokee County, N.C., 13 October 1984.

44. Tape recorded interview with Monroe Ledford, Union community, Macon County, N.C., 21 October 1983.

45. French Haynes interview. Despite the fact that she reported that the homeplace usually went to the youngest boy, Miss Haynes, the only girl of seven children, inherited her own homeplace. The preference for the home to go to an unmarried child, particularly a girl, is strong although it is seldom explicitly stated.

46. For example, Maudine Martin, who is unmarried, stayed on at her homeplace (the Cornelius Gentile Price House). She reported, however, that it was owned by the "heirs." Interview with Maudine Martin, Bell View community, Cherokee County, N.C., 22 June 1981.

47. Robert Blanton interview; Bass Hyatt interview; and tape recorded interview with Eula Sheffield Bryson, Cowee community, Macon County, N.C., 12 October 1983.

48. Zena Bennett interview.

49. Tape recorded interview with Leslie Ward, Wayehutta community, Jackson County, N.C., 13 September 1983.

50. Robert Blanton interview.

51. Bessie Tilley interview.

52. Robert Blanton interview.

53. Oma Jenkins interview.

54. Leslie Ward interview.
55. Zena Bennett interview.
56. Essie Moore interview.
57. Eula Bryson interview.
58. Interview with H. L. Martin, Martin's Creek, Cherokee County, N.C., 26 June 1981.
59. Tom Adler's study of folk housing in the east-central Blue Ridge explores similar uses and attitudes. Adler cites the example of a man in Allegheny County, North Carolina, who values an old house but also uses it to store hay. Although the building is decrepit, he adamantly refuses to sell it. Adler suggests, "An old house may functionally become a barn; but in memory it always remains a house." Adler, "Toward an Ecology of Folk Housing in the East-Central Blue Ridge," pp. 27–28.
60. Tape recorded interview with Eller Garrett, Unaka community, Cherokee County, N.C., 20 June 1984.
61. Minnie McDonald interview.

Conclusion

1. The best example of this approach is Martin, *Hollybush*.
2. Martin, *Hollybush*; Pocius, "Calvert"; and Glassie, *Passing the Time in Ballymenone*.
3. Tape recorded interview with Frances Bryson, Cowee community, Macon County, N.C., 26 July 1984; tape recorded interview with Nanny Potts Sorrells, Cowee community, Macon County, N.C., 12 October 1983; tape recorded interview with Vinnie Matlock McGaha, Cowee community, Macon County, N.C., 12 October 1983; tape recorded interview with Eula Sheffield Bryson, Cowee community, Macon County, N.C., 12 October 1983; tape recorded interview with Leo Gibson, Cowee community, Macon County, N.C., 12 October 1983; and tape recorded interview with Katherine Porter, Rose Creek, Macon County, N.C., 3 August 1984.
4. Interview with Jess Ledford, Bryson City, Swain County, N.C., 7 August 1984; interview with George Woodard, Bryson City, Swain County, N.C., 7 August 1984; and tape recorded interview with Robert Blanton, Matlock Creek, Macon County, N.C., 3 July 1984.

5. For comparative data see Martin, *Hollybush*, and Adler, "Toward an Ecology of Folk Housing in the East-Central Blue Ridge." My own fieldwork in northeastern Mississippi suggests the widespread distribution of certain spatial patterns throughout the Upland South.

6. Although George McDaniel suggests some syncretism between African and Anglo-American traditions in the folk building by Maryland blacks, the evidence on spatial patterns is suggestive of the adoption of many Anglo-American patterns of architectural use. This is very different from the strong retention of African spatial patterns indicated by John Michael Vlach, "Sources of the Shotgun House: African and Caribbean Antecedents for Afro-American Architecture" (Ph.D. dissertation, Indiana University, 1975), and Joyner, *Down by the Riverside*, pp. 117–26. This difference is perhaps attributable to the very different historical experience of blacks in coastal South Carolina and Louisiana from that of black Marylanders. See McDaniel, *Hearth and Home*.

7. This would include specific regional patterns in post-medieval England, seventeenth- and early eighteenth-century New England and the tidewater South, and early to mid-twentieth-century Northern Ireland.

8. Even in New England there is evidence for the maintenance of conservative spatial patterns among some rural people into the nineteenth century. See Hubka, *Big House, Little House, Back House, Barn*, pp. 34–54; and Cummings, *The Framed Houses of Massachusetts Bay*, p. 28.

9. Henry Glassie, "Folkloristic Study of the American Artifact," in *Handbook of American Folklore*, ed. Richard M. Dorson (Bloomington: Indiana University Press, 1983), p. 377.

10. See Christian Norberg-Schulz, *Intentions in Architecture* (Cambridge: M.I.T. Press, 1965), pp. 109–30. Norberg-Schulz's division of building tasks is similar to the three levels of functions of artifacts (technomic, sociotechnic, and ideo-technic) suggested by Lewis Binford. See Lewis Binford, "Archaeology as Anthropology," *American Antiquity* 28 (Oct. 1962): 217–26, and James Deetz, *In Small Things Forgotten: The Archeology of Early American Life* (Garden City, N.Y.: Anchor Press, Doubleday, 1977), p. 51.

11. Amos Rapoport, *House Form and Culture* (Englewood Cliffs, N.J.: Prentice-Hall, 1969), p. 47; Peirce F. Lewis, "Common Housing, Cultural Spoor," *Landscape* 19 (January 1975): 2; and Glassie, *Folk Housing in Middle Virginia*, p. 138.

12. Vlach, "Sources of the Shotgun House," p. 194.

13. Joyner, *Down by the Riverside*, pp. 117–26.

14. See Glassie, *Folk Housing in Middle Virginia*.

15. Dell Hymes, *Foundations in Sociolinguistics: An Ethnographic Approach* (Philadelphia: University of Pennsylvania Press, 1974), p. 9.

16. See Michael Ann Williams, "The Realm of the Tangible: A Folklorist's Role in Architectural Documentation and Preservation," in *The Conservation of Culture: Folklorists and the Public Sector*, ed. Burt Feintuch (Lexington: University Press of Kentucky, 1988), pp. 196–205.

17. Upton, "Vernacular Domestic Architecture in Eighteenth Century Virginia," p. 82.

18. Upton, "Vernacular Domestic Architecture in Eighteenth Century Virginia," p. 108. Glassie, *Passing the Time in Ballymenone*, p. 327.

19. Cary Carson suggests for historically oriented material culture studies that the artifact contributes most to social history when it is part of the subject of study rather than just evidence. See Cary Carson, "Doing History with Material Culture," in *Material Culture and the Study of American Life*, ed. Ian M. G. Quimby (New York: W. W. Norton & Co., for the Henry Francis du Pont Winterthur Museum, 1978), pp. 41–68.

20. Bachelard, *The Poetics of Space*, pp. 47–48.

21. Bill Hillier and Julienne Hanson, *The Social Logic of Space* (Cambridge: Cambridge University Press, 1984), p. 1.

BIBLIOGRAPHY

Published Works

Adler, Elizabeth Mosby. "Personalization and Conformity in Expansion Architecture." *Material Culture* 19 (1987): 127–38.

Ashcraft, Norman, and Albert E. Scheflen, *People Space: The Making and Breaking of Human Boundaries*. Garden City, N.Y.: Anchor Books, 1976.

Bachelard, Gaston. *The Poetics of Space*. Translated by Maria Jolas. Boston: Beacon Press, 1969.

Barley, M. W. *The English Farmhouse and Cottage*. London: Routledge and Kegan Paul, 1961.

Barley, Maurice. "A Glossary of Names for Rooms in Houses of the Sixteenth and Seventeenth Centuries." In *Culture and Environment: Essays in Honour of Sir Cyril Fox*, edited by I. L. L. Foster and L. Alcock, pp. 479–501. London: Routledge and Kegan Paul, 1963.

Barthes, Roland. "Historical Discourse." In *Structuralism: A Reader*, edited by Michael Lane, pp. 145–55. London: Jonathan Cape, 1970.

Bartram, William. *Travels Through North and South Carolina, Georgia, East and West Florida*. Facsimile of 1792 London Edition. Savannah, Ga.: Beehive Press, 1973.

Beaver, Patricia Duane. *Rural Community in the Appalachian South*. Lexington: University Press of Kentucky, 1986.

Binford, Lewis. "Archaeology as Anthropology." *American Antiquity* 28 (Oct. 1962): 217–26.

Blackmun, Ora. *Western North Carolina: Its Mountains and Its People to 1880*. Boone, N.C.: Appalachian Consortium Press, 1977.

Blethen, Tyler, and Curtis Wood Jr. *From Ulster to Carolina: The Migration of the Scotch-Irish to Southwestern North Carolina*. Cullowhee, N.C.: Western Carolina University, 1983.

Bronner, Simon. "Manner Books and Suburban Houses: The Structure of Traditional Aesthetics." *Winterthur Portfolio* 18 (Spring 1983): 61–68.

Brunskill, R. W. *Illustrated Handbook of Vernacular Architecture*. 2d ed. Boston: Faber and Faber, 1978.

———. *Vernacular Architecture of the Lake Counties*. Boston: Faber and Faber, Faber Paperback Edition, 1978.

Bryant, F. Carlene. *We're All Kin: A Cultural Study of a Mountain Neighborhood*. Knoxville: University of Tennessee Press, 1981.

Carson, Cary. "Doing History with Material Culture." In *Material Culture and the Study of American Life*, edited by Ian M. G. Quimby, pp. 41–64. New York: W. W. Norton & Co., for the Henry Francis du Pont Winterthur Museum, 1978.

Carson, Cary, Norman F. Barka, William M. Kelso, Gary Wheeler Stone and Dell Upton. "Impermanent Architecture in the Southern American Colonies." *Winterthur Portfolio* 16 (1981): 135–96.

Carter, Thomas. " 'It Was in the Way, So We Took It Out': Remodeling as Social Commentary." *Material Culture* 19 (1987): 113–25.

Cassidy, Frederic G. *Dictionary of American Regional English*. Volume 1, *Introduction and A–C*. Cambridge: Harvard University Press, Belknap Press, 1985.

Christensen, Anne Louise Gjesdal. "Dwellings as Communication." *Ethnologia Scandinavica* 9 (1979): 68–88.

Craigie, Sir William A., ed. *A Dictionary of the Older Scottish Tongue from the Twelfth Century to the End of the Seventeenth*. Volume 1, *A–C*. Chicago: University of Chicago Press, 1937.

Cromley, Elizabeth Collins. "Modernization; Or, 'You Never See a Screen Door on Affluent Homes.' " *Journal of American Culture* 5, no. 2 (Summer 1982): 71–79.

Csikszentmihalyi, Mihaly, and Eugene Rochberg-Halton. *The Meaning of Things: Domestic Symbols and Self*. Cambridge: Cambridge University Press, 1981.

Cummings, Abbott Lowell. *The Framed Houses of Massachusetts Bay, 1625–1725*. Cambridge: Harvard University Press, Belknap Press, 1979.

Deetz, James. *In Small Things Forgotten: The Archeology of Early American Life*. Garden City, N.Y.: Anchor Press, Doubleday, 1977.

Demos, John. *A Little Commonwealth: Family Life in Plymouth Colony*. New York: Oxford University Press, 1970.

Dickens, Roy S., Jr. *Cherokee Prehistory: The Pisgah Phase in the Appalachian Summit Region*. Knoxville: University of Tennessee Press, 1976.

Dorson, Richard M. "Oral Tradition and Written History: The Case for the United States." *Journal of the Folklore Institute* 1 (1964): 220–34.

Douglas, Mary. "Symbolic Orders in the Use of Domestic Space." In *Man, Settlement, and Urbanism*, edited by Peter J. Ucko, Ruth Tringham, and G. W. Dimbleby, pp. 513–21. London: Duckworth, 1972.

Eller, Ronald D. *Miners, Millhands, and Mountaineers: Industrialization of the Appalachian South, 1880–1930*. Knoxville: University of Tennessee Press, 1982.

Faulds, Sara Salene. " 'The Spaces in Which We Live': The Role of Folkloristics in the Urban Design Process." *Folklore and Mythology Studies* 5 (1981): 48–59.

Flaherty, David H. *Privacy in Colonial New England*. Charlottesville: University Press of Virginia, 1972.

Freel, Margaret Walker. *Our Heritage: The People of Cherokee County, North Carolina*. Asheville, N.C.: Miller Printing Company, 1956.

Glassie, Henry. "Eighteenth-Century Cultural Process in Delaware Valley Folk Building." *Winterthur Portfolio* 7 (1972): 29–57.

———. *Folk Housing in Middle Virginia: A Structural Analysis of Historic Artifacts*. Knoxville: University of Tennessee Press, 1975.

———. "Folkloristic Study of the American Artifact." In *Handbook of American Folklore*, edited by Richard M. Dorson, pp. 376–83. Bloomington: Indiana University Press, 1983.

———. *Passing the Time in Ballymenone: Culture and History of an Ulster Community*. Philadelphia: University of Pennsylvania Press, 1982.

———. "The Types of the Southern Mountain Cabin." In *The Study of American Folklore*, edited by Jan Brunvand, pp. 338–70. New York: W. W. Norton & Co., 1968.

Goffman, Erving. *The Presentation of Self in Everyday Life*. Garden City, N.Y.: Doubleday, Anchor Books, 1959.

Hall, Edward T. *The Hidden Dimension*. Garden City, N.Y.: Doubleday, 1966.

Herman, Bernard L. "Architectural Renewal and the Maintenance of Customary Relationships." *Material Culture* 19 (1987): 85–99.

Hillier, Bill, and Julienne Hanson. *The Social Logic of Space*. Cambridge: Cambridge University Press, 1984.

Howell, Benita J. *A Survey of Folklife Along the Big South Fork of the Cumberland River*. Report of Investigations, No. 30. Department of Anthropology, University of Tennessee, Knoxville, 1981.

Hubka, Thomas C. *Big House, Little House, Back House, Barn: The Connected Farm Buildings of New England*. Hanover: University Press of New England, 1984.

———. "The Connected Farm Buildings of Southwestern Maine." *Pioneer America* 9 (1977): 143–78.

Hudson, Charles. "Folk History and Ethnohistory." *Ethnohistory* 13 (1966): 52–70.

Hurst, J. G. "The Changing Medieval Village in England." In *Man, Settlement, and Urbanism*, edited by Peter J. Ucko, Ruth Tringham, and G. W. Dimbleby, pp. 531–40. London: Duckworth, 1972.

Hymes, Dell. *Foundations in Sociolinguistics: An Ethnographic Approach*. Philadelphia: University of Pennsylvania Press, 1974.

Inscoe, John C. "Mountain Masters: Slaveholding in Western North Carolina." *North Carolina Historical Review* 60 (1983): 143–73.

Jones, Michael Owen. "L.A. Add-ons and Re-dos: Renovation in Folk Art and Architectural Design." In *Perspectives on American Folk Art*, edited by Ian M. G. Quimby and Scott T. Swank, pp. 325–63. New York: W. W. Norton, 1980.

Jordan, Terry G. *American Log Buildings: An Old World Heritage*. Chapel Hill: University of North Carolina Press, 1985.

Joyner, Charles. *Down by the Riverside: A South Carolina Slave Community*. Urbana and Chicago: University of Illinois Press, 1984.

Keel, Bennie C. *Cherokee Archaeology: A Study of the Appalachian Summit*. Knoxville: University of Tennessee Press, 1976.

Kent, Susan. *Analyzing Activity Areas: An Ethnoarchaeological Study of the Use of Space*. Albuquerque: University of New Mexico Press, 1984.

Kniffen, Fred. "Folk Housing: Key to Diffusion." *Annals of the Association of American Geographers* 55 (December 1955): 549–77.

Kurath, Hans. *A Word Geography of the Eastern United States*. Ann Arbor: University of Michigan Press, 1949.

Lewis, Peirce F. "Common Housing, Cultural Spoor." *Landscape* 19 (January 1975): 1–22.

Lounsbury, Carl. "The Development of Domestic Architecture in the Albemarle Region." In *Carolina Dwelling*, edited by Doug Swaim, pp. 46–61. Student Publication of the School of Design, Volume 26. Raleigh: North Carolina State University, 1978.

McDaniel, George W. *Hearth and Home: Preserving a People's Culture*. Philadelphia: Temple University Press, 1982.

Madden, Robert R., and T. Russell Jones. *Mountain Home—The Walker Family Homestead*. Washington, D.C.: U.S. Department of Interior, 1977.

Martin, Charles E. *Hollybush: Folk Building and Social Change in an Appalachian Community*. Knoxville: University of Tennessee Press, 1984.

Milspaw, Yvonne J. "Reshaping Tradition: Changes to Pennsylvania German Folk Houses." *Pioneer America: The Journal of Historic Material Culture* 15, no. 2 (July 1983): 67–84.

Moe, John F. "Concepts of Shelter: The Folk Poetics of Space, Change, and Continuity." *Journal of Popular Culture* 11 (1977): 219–53.

Nelson, Walter R. "Some Examples of Plank House Construction and Their Origin." *Pioneer America* 1 (July 1969): 18–29.

Noble, Allen G. *Wood, Brick, and Stone: The North American Settlement Landscape*. Volume 1, *Houses*. Amherst: University of Massachusetts Press, 1984.

Norberg-Schulz, Christian. *Existence, Space, and Architecture*. New York: Praeger, 1971.

———. *Intentions in Architecture*. Cambridge: M.I.T. Press, 1965.

Perdue, Charles L., Jr., and Nancy J. Martin-Perdue, "Appalachian Fables and Facts: A Case Study of the Shenandoah National Park Removals." *Appalachian Journal* 7 (Autumn–Winter 1979–80): 84–104.

Pocius, Gerald L. "Raised Roofs and High Hopes: Rebuildings on Newfoundland's Southern Shore." *Material Culture* 19 (1987): 67–84.

Rapoport, Amos. *House Form and Culture*. Englewood Cliffs, N.J.: Prentice-Hall, 1969.

Rybczynski, Witold. *Home: A Short History of an Idea*. New York: Viking, 1986.

Sommer, Robert. *Personal Space: The Behavorial Basis of Design*. Englewood Cliffs, N.J.: Prentice-Hall, 1969.

Southern, Kathleen Pepi. *Historic Preservation in Rural North Carolina: Problems and Potentials*. Raleigh: Historic Preservation Society of North Carolina, 1982.

Southern, Michael. "The I-House as a Carrier of Style in Three Counties of the Northeastern Piedmont." In *Carolina Dwelling*, edited by Doug Swaim, pp. 70–83. Student Publication of the School of Design, Volume 26. Raleigh: North Carolina State University, 1978.

Stahl, Sandra K. D. "The Oral Personal Narrative in Its Generic Context." *Fabula* 18 (1977): 18–39.

Swaim, Douglas. *Cabins and Castles: The History and Architecture of Buncombe County, North Carolina*. Asheville: Historic Resources Commission of Asheville and Buncombe County, 1981.

Tuan, Yi-Fu. *Man and Nature*. Commission on College Geography, Resource Paper, No. 10. Washington, D.C.: Association of American Geographers, 1971.

———. *Space and Place: The Perspective of Experience*. Minneapolis: University of Minnesota Press, 1977.

Upton, Dell. "Toward a Performance Theory of Vernacular Architecture: Early Tidewater Virginia as a Case Study." *Folklore Forum* 12 (1979): 173–96.

———. "Traditional Timber Framing." In *Material Culture of the Wooden Age*, edited by Brooke Hindle, pp. 35–93. Tarrytown, N.Y.: Sleepy Hollow Press, 1981.

———. "Vernacular Domestic Architecture in Eighteenth Century Virginia." *Winterthur Portfolio* 17 (Summer/Autumn 1982): 95–119.

Van Noppen, Ina Woestenmeyer, and John J. Van Noppen, *Western North Carolina Since the Civil War*. Boone, N.C.: Appalachian Consortium Press, 1973.

Wenger, Mark R. "The Central Passage in Virginia: Evolution of Eighteenth-Century Living Space." In *Perspectives in Vernacular Architecture, II*, edited by Camille Wells, pp. 137–49. Columbia: University of Missouri Press, 1986.

White, Hayden. "Interpretation in History." *New Literary History* 4 (1973): 281–314.

Williams, Michael Ann. *Marble and Log: The History and Architecture of Cherokee County, North Carolina*. Murphy, N.C.: Cherokee County Historical Museum Council, 1984.

———. "The Realm of the Tangible: A Folklorist's Role in Architectural Documentation and Preservation." In *The Conservation of Culture: Folklorists
and the Public Sector*, edited by Burt Feintuch. Lexington: University Press
of Kentucky, 1988.

Wilson, Eugene M. *Alabama Folk Houses*. Montgomery: Alabama Historical
Commission, 1975.

Wright, Joseph. *The English Dialect Dictionary*. Oxford: Henry Frowde, 1905.

Wright, Martin. "The Antecedents of the Double Pen House Type." *Annals of
the Association of American Geographers* 48, no. 2 (1958): 109–17.

Unpublished Works

Adler, Thomas A. "Toward an Ecology of Folk Housing in the East-Central
Blue Ridge." Unpublished manuscript submitted to the American Folklife
Center, Library of Congress, Washington, D.C.

Bergengren, Charles. "The Cycle of Transformations in Schaefferstown, Pennsylvania, Houses." Paper presented to the annual meeting of the Vernacular
Architecture Forum, May 1988.

Cashion, Jerry Clyde. "Fort Butler and the Cherokee Indian Removal from
North Carolina." Draft report prepared for the North Carolina State Division
of Archives and History, 1970.

Cotton, J. Randall. "The Built Environment of Haywood County." Unpublished
report on file at North Carolina Division of Archives and History, Western
Office, Asheville, North Carolina.

Owen, Margaret Counts. "The Historic Architectural Resources of Western
North Carolina: A Ten County Reconnaissance Survey and Preliminary
Analysis." Unpublished report, on file at North Carolina Division of Archives
and History, Western Office, Asheville, North Carolina.

Pocius, Gerald Lewis. "Calvert: A Study of Artifacts and Spatial Usage in a
Newfoundland Community." Ph.D. dissertation, University of Pennsylvania, 1979.

———. "Privacy and Architecture: A Newfoundland Example." Paper presented to the annual meeting of the Vernacular Architecture Forum, Salt Lake
City, Utah, May 1987.

St. George, Robert Blair. "A Retreat from the Wilderness: Pattern in the

Domestic Environments of Southeastern New England, 1630–1730." Ph.D. dissertation, University of Pennsylvania, 1982.

Vlach, John Michael. "Sources of the Shotgun House: African and Caribbean Antecedents for Afro-American Architecture." Ph.D. dissertation, Indiana University, 1975.

Williams, Michael Ann. "The Architecture of Henderson County, North Carolina." Unpublished report, on file at North Carolina Division of Archives and History, Western Office, Asheville, North Carolina.

————. "The Use of Vernacular Architecture in the Rural South: Some Observations and Directions for Further Research." Unpublished manuscript.

Woody, Jonathan. Oral interview, conducted by George Richardson and Sam Easterby. Waynesville, Haywood County, North Carolina. 27 February 1973. Transcript located in North Carolina Collection, Haywood County Public Library, Waynesville, North Carolina.

Archival and Photographic Collections

Great Smoky Mountains National Park, Sugarlands Visitor Center. Photographic archives.

Haywood County Public Library, Waynesville, North Carolina. North Carolina Collection.

North Carolina Division of Archives and History, Western Office, Asheville, North Carolina. County files.

Post-Survey Interviews

Arms, Tiny. Owl Creek community, Cherokee County, N.C. 10 July 1984. Tape recorded.

Bennett, Zena. Iotla community, Macon County, N.C. 18 October 1983. Tape recorded.

Blanton, Robert. Matlock Creek, Macon County, N.C. 3 July 1984. Tape recorded.

Bryson, Eula Sheffield. Cowee community, Macon County, N.C. 12 October 1983. Tape recorded.

Bryson, Frances. Cowee community, Macon County, N.C. 26 July 1984. Tape recorded.

Caldwell, Pearl. Maggie Valley, Haywood County, N.C. 24 July 1984. Tape recorded.

Carringer, Grady. Stecoah community, Graham County, N.C. 14 September 1984. Tape recorded.

Cochran, Vestal. Nantahala community, Macon County, N.C. 26 June 1984. Tape recorded.

Collett, Anna. Valleytown community, Cherokee County, N.C. 13 October 1983. Tape recorded.

Dean, Lolita. Burningtown community, Macon County, N.C. 10 August 1984. Tape recorded.

Fisher, Charlie. Addie community, Jackson County, N.C. 28 August 1984. Tape recorded.

Fisher, Fanny. Addie community, Jackson County, N.C. 28 August 1984. Tape recorded.

Frady, Mary. Cowee community, Macon County, N.C. 12 October 1983. Tape recorded.

Frazier, Jessie. Cullowhee, Jackson County, N.C. 21 July 1984. Tape recorded.

Gaddis, Loomis. Boiling Springs community, Cherokee County, N.C. 21 June 1984. Tape recorded.

Garrett, Eller. Unaka community, Cherokee County, N.C. 20 June 1984. Tape recorded.

Gibson, Leo. Cowee community, Macon County, N.C. 12 October 1983. Tape recorded.

Greene, Arvel. Wilmont, Jackson County, N.C. 18 June 1984. Tape recorded.

Gunter, Larry. Ninevah community, Haywood County, N.C. 31 August 1984. Tape recorded.

Gunter, Quincy. Ninevah community, Haywood County, N.C. 31 August 1984. Tape recorded.

Haynes, French. Clyde, Haywood County, N.C. 25 July 1984. Tape recorded.

Hicks, Letha. Big Bend community, Haywood County, N.C. 8 September 1984. Tape recorded.

Hyatt, Bass. Brasstown, Clay County, N.C. 21 September 1984. Tape recorded.

Hyatt, Lucy Moore. Brasstown, Clay County, N.C. 21 September 1984. Tape recorded.

Jenkins, Oma. Stecoah community, Graham County, N.C. 23 May 1984. Tape recorded.

Ledford, Jess. Bryson City, Swain County, N.C. 7 August 1984.

Ledford, Monroe. Union community, Macon County, N.C. 21 October 1983. Tape recorded.

McDonald, Minnie. Hanging Dog community, Cherokee County, N.C. 27 August 1984. Tape recorded.

McGaha, Vinnie Matlock. Cowee community, Macon County, N.C. 12 October 1983. Tape recorded.

Messer, Bertha. Cowee community, Macon County, N.C. 7 July 1984. Tape recorded.

Messer, Frank. West Waynesville, Haywood County, N.C. 6 September 1984. Tape recorded.

Messer, Mary. West Waynesville, Haywood County, N.C. 6 September 1984. Tape recorded.

Moody, Nora. Iotla community, Macon County, N.C. 24 September 1984. Tape recorded.

Moore, Essie. Caney Fork community, Jackson County, N.C. 5 September 1984. Tape recorded.

Neal, Jane. Aquone community, Macon County, N.C. 2 August 1984. Tape recorded.

Neal, Jim. Aquone community, Macon County, N.C. 2 August 1984. Tape recorded.

Norton, Addie. Otto community, Macon County, N.C. 18 July 1984. Tape recorded.

Porter, Katherine. Rose Creek community, Macon County, N.C. 3 August 1984. Tape recorded.

Pressley, Willa Mae. Bo Cove community, Jackson County, N.C. 28 June 1984. Tape recorded.

Queen, Mary Jane. John's Creek community, Jackson County, N.C. 24 August 1984. Tape recorded.

Rogers, Kate. Ellijay community, Macon County, N.C. 3 October 1983, 17 July 1984. Tape recorded.

Rogers, Mike. Anderson Branch community, Graham County, N.C. 27 January 1984. Tape recorded.

Sorrells, Nanny Potts. Cowee community, Macon County, N.C. 12 October 1983. Tape recorded.

Tilley, Bessie. Tilley Creek, Jackson County, N.C. 9 July 1984. Tape recorded.

Wallin, Berzilla. Sodom-Laurel community, Madison County, N.C. 28 July 1984. Tape recorded.

Ward, Leslie. Wayehutta community, Jackson County, N.C. 13 September 1984. Tape recorded.

Ward, Lois. Bryson City, Swain County, N.C. 7 August 1984.

Williams, Gilford. Stecoah community, Graham County, N.C. 4 October 1983. Tape recorded.

Wilson, R. O. Wilson Creek, Jackson County, N.C. 5 October 1983. Tape recorded.

Woodard, George. Bryson City, Swain County, N.C. 7 August 1984.

Survey Interviews

Conversations with a large number of individuals during the Henderson County and Cherokee County surveys shaped the nature of this study. Only those interviews specifically cited in the study are included here.

Justus, Ernest. Upward community, Henderson County, N.C. 13 August 1980.

McGuire, Polly Stewart. Andrews, Cherokee County, N.C. 25 August 1981.

Martin, H. L. Martin's Creek, Cherokee County, N.C. 26 June 1981.

Martin, Maudine. Bell View community, Cherokee County, N.C. 22 June 1981.

Stirewalt, R. Ranger community, Cherokee County, N.C. 2 November 1981.

INDEX